The Simple Way To Success

The Simple Way To Success

Larry H. Winget

The Simple Way To Success

Larry Winget

Published by:

Win Publications!
a subsidiary of Win Seminars!, Inc.
P. O. Box 700485
Tulsa, Oklahoma 74170

The Simple Way To Success
was previously published as
The Ya Gotta's For Success!

Order information:

800 749-4597

www.larrywinget.com

Printed in the United States of America.
Cover design and layout by Ad Graphics, Tulsa, Oklahoma.
Library of Congress Catalog Number: 96-90143
ISBN 1-881342-12-3

10 9 8 7 6 5 4 3 2 1

Also By
Larry Winget

That Makes Me Sick!

The Simple Way To Success

Money Is Easy

Stuff That Works Every Single Day

The Little Red Book Of Stuff That Works

Profound Stuff

Success One Day At A Time

Just Do This Stuff

How To Write A Book One Page At A Time

The Wit And Wisdom Of Larry Winget

Anthologies:
Only The Best On Success
Only The Best On Leadership
Only The Best On Customer Service
Outlaw Wisdom
The Outlaws Of Success

For a complete catalog of
Larry's books, audio and video systems, and other
unique personal and professional development
products including UNGAWA GEAR™
sportwear, call:
800 749-4597
www.larrywinget.com

Contents

Dedication

To my Mom and Dad, who taught me to always believe in myself and my abilities; to expect the best from myself and others; to trust God; to love life and to live it for all it's worth.

To my wonderful wife Rose Mary, who has always been my biggest fan and supporter; and who believed in me even when I forgot to.

To my boys, Tyler and Patrick, who help me keep it all in perspective.

Before you begin . . .

This is **your** book. It is **personal** and **private**. Write in it and mark in it and underline it and highlight it. I want you to. I also suggest that you not loan it to anyone or even let others look at it when you've finished. Buy them their own copy.

Each chapter has a place for you to make notes and some of the chapters will ask you to write down a specific action step. Do it. It will increase your ability to gain from the information. Confucius said many years ago that what you hear you will forget; what you hear and see you will remember; but what you hear, see and experience will become a part of you. Please **experience** this book by writing in it and involving yourself in the action steps that follow the chapters.

Caution: Some of the action steps take a great deal of thought and consideration. Take all of the time you need, but don't get bogged down. If you allow yourself to get stuck, your success might lose momemtum. So keep moving!

Now get your highlighter and pen and get started!

Introduction

This book is for those who want to be successful and need some help figuring out what success is and what it takes to get there. And it's for those who consider themselves successful and yet are still saying that there simply must be more to it than this! It is also for those people who have attended the "how-to" workshops and seminars and read the "how-to" books and listened to the "how-to" tapes and they still don't know "how-to" be a success. And it's for those people who know the techniques, have the skills and have the knowledge from a "how-to" standpoint and still aren't "there."

I have been in all of those positions. I was once one of those who had been to the seminars and read the books and listened to the tapes and was still not where they promised I would be. At that point I became once again one of those trying to define success and attempting to determine my own personal path to get there. Finally, there was the point where I thought that I had made it only to find out that there was so much I was still missing.

Specific circumstances have brought me to where I am today.

A few years ago I was working for AT&T and decided to take an early retirement package that was offered shortly after the deregulation of the Bell System. I moved back to my native Oklahoma and decided to open my own business selling business telephone systems. I didn't have any money to start a business . . . I just started. I started with a technician, a secretary and me. Very soon I experienced incredible success through the tremendous growth opportunities found in the telecommunications industry at that time.

My small company grew in five years to become the second largest independent telecommunications company in the state. I had over thirty people on the payroll; big beautiful offices; a fleet of trucks. I was doing well financially and felt fairly successful. I served on the "right" civic committees, and traveled in the "right" social circles. By most standards, I was doing all right. That's when it all happened. Everything came crashing in around me. I made some terrible errors in judgement and in trust. The business failed. I lost my employees, my business and all of my money. The business filed bankruptcy and because I was the owner and president, I had signed personally for everything and was financially responsible for it all. I was forced to file bankruptcy too. This was the most personally devastating thing I had ever been through. I was raised to believe that you pay your debts and that people who went bankrupt were either deadbeats or crooks or had no respect for themselves or their obligations. But there I was, one of them. Since both my wife and I worked for our company we lost all of our income stream. I was so embarrassed that I dropped out of all of the civic and social activities I was involved in and just knew that everyone in the world would think that I was a bad person.

It was in the midst of all of this trouble, all of this mess, all of this so-called failure that I discovered success. It was during this time that I realized what success really is. I had heard for years that success was not the destination, but the journey. I had also heard it said that it is not what you get by reaching your goals, but what you become on the way to your goals. And while I had heard all of those things, I somehow hadn't allowed it all to sink in. But at that dark moment in time for me it all began to register. It seems ironic that a person can finally understand success in the middle of failure, but that is exactly what happened.

Allow me to make something perfectly clear. This was both the worst and the best thing that could have ever happened to me. Looking back at it all now I know that I created the business failure. Not on purpose, but it did happen as a result of my thinking and my actions. And it allowed me to become the person I was meant to be and pursue the career that I had always dreamed of. It also prepared me for that career and strengthened my message. So while it was the **worst** thing that ever happened to me, it was definitely the **best** thing that ever happened to me

Maybe you have had a similar experience. Even if you didn't own a business that failed and you didn't end up in bankruptcy, I'm sure that you've had disappointments. We have all had disappointments.

I have a good friend who was laid off of his job after nearly 20 years of service to the company. It seemed like a terrible thing at the time. But eventually it turned out to be very positive because it forced him to make changes in his attitude about himself and his abilities. The end result was that he found a career in a totally different field and is very happy, satisfied and successful at it. That became his "worst/best" experience.

Maybe you have had a "worst/best" experience. Something that in retrospect turned your life around. Something that grabbed you by the collar and slapped you silly and later turned out to be a tremendously positive thing. Or maybe you've had a "worst" thing and need to look back at it in order to find the "best" that came about as a result of it.

That's what brought me to recognize the need for this book. Because I'm convinced that there are many of you who want to know what success is and what you can do about getting some of it. And I'll just bet that there are plenty of you who have been to seminars, bought the books and tapes and still aren't where you want to be. If so, this is the right book for you. Because in this book you're going to find out what I did to turn it all around. You'll also find the information that will help you to become the success that you were meant to be.

The principles that I'm offering you here are sound, ethical, smart, and rewarding. However, there are no guarantees. *The Simple Way To Success* is **not** a magic formula. To tell you that I have mastered all of these qualities would be a lie. To tell you that I have everything in life I want as a result of using these principles would also be a lie. These principles are the ones that brought me through my struggles and are working for me on my way to where I want to be. I know that they will help you regardless of where you have been, where you are, or where you are going.

Start the journey toward success by identifying your "worst/ best" experience. Write it here. Doing so will help you begin to focus on the possibilities in you and your experiences.

Chapter One

Success

Success: A confusing term. You can go to the bookstore and buy five hundred books on success by people telling you that only **they** have the true key to success. I've heard many speakers give their ideas on the keys to success. I've heard them say things like "the key to success is hard work; there's just no substitute for hard work." I've heard them say "the key to success is knowledge. The more you know the greater your chances of being successful." I've heard sales trainers say that "the key to success in sales is to learn all of the techniques, all of the great openers and the tricky closes, and then you'll be successful in sales." I've heard them say that "the key to success in business is learning to negotiate. If you can just learn to negotiate, then success is just around the corner." I've listened to the guys on TV that come on late at night tell us that if we'll just buy their books and tapes and then buy all of the distressed property in the world, we are bound to become millionaires. (I wonder if that means we'll get one of those Hawaiian shirts in the package too?) I've been told that if you'll just sell this nutritional supplement or this line of soap product to your friends then financial success will be yours. I've heard coaches say "just practice, practice, practice, and then you'll be successful."

They all make it sound so simple! And it is! That's the good news. Success is simple. But not in the way you normally hear. It's not about get rich quick schemes or in this bit of trickery or that. It's not about slick moves. It's about following principles. Principles that are profoundly simple. Principles that are so simple that most of us overlook them. That's really what this book is. It's just a group of simple principles that when followed will allow you to achieve the level of success you desire.

So what **is** success? I found through my personal experience that success is more than money and more than cars and "stuff." I also found that success starts with what you **are**, not what you **do**, or what you **have.** Success is the journey and not the destination. It is the joy and inner peace you have in the presence of suffering. It is being thankful for what you have while you pursue having more. It is opening your eyes to the serendipitous moments of life that surround us. It is health, family, and love. It is the excitement of looking for the good and not dwelling on the bad. It is balance between all of the areas of your life. It is..

The list can go on and on . . . and should. However, those are my personal ideas of success. Let's look at others:

To laugh often and much; to win the respect of intelligent people and the affection of children; to earn the appreciation of honest critics and endure the betrayal of false friends; to appreciate beauty; to find the best in others; to leave the world a bit better, whether by a healthy child, a garden patch or a redeemed social condition; to know even one life has breathed easier because you lived. This is to have succeeded!

—Ralph Waldo Emerson

Success is the progressive realization of a worthy ideal.

—Earl Nightingale

Those are two of my favorite definitions of success. Now I'll give you mine:

> **!** "Success is being all you can be in each area of your life without sacrificing your ability to be all you can be in each and every other area of your life."

Let me explain exactly what I mean. I say that you have to be all you can be. That means being your very best. It doesn't say $100,000 per year or a million dollars a year, or a new Mercedes every year or able to run a marathon when you are 65 years old or having five homes around the world or living to be 100 years old. It says be your best. Not by my standards or anyone else's standards, but by your own standards. That's what really counts. Your best. I have no amounts in my definition. That because amounts are never enough and never a good way to determine ultimate success. **Only your best is ever enough.**

My definition also addresses balance. While I will spend more time on the subject of balance in another chapter, I want to emphasize here that balance is critical to success. Your life has many areas: Career/Business, Social/Civic, Financial, Family, Physical/Health, Mental/Continuing Education and Spiritual. They are all important. None can be left out or sacrificed in any way to have total success. I believe that it is our obligation to be our best in each of these areas, never sacrificing one while pursuing another.

That's my definition. We all need one. So I want you to write yours. Remember this is **your** book. Write in it, underline it, mark it up in any way that makes it more meaningful to you. It is very important to have a succinct idea of what success means to you. It is your mission statement. You wouldn't consider working for a company that didn't have a mission statement: a clearly defined purpose for being. You know that a company without a mission statement could never be successful. How can you consider living a successful life without a clearly defined purpose for being? That's what your personal definition of success will be for you.

My personal definition of success:

Chapter Two

Take Responsibility

We are all self-made; but only the successful will admit it.

Earl Nightingale

Success is 99% luck. Ask any failure.

Unknown

When you miss the target, never in history has it been the target's fault.

Unknown

Taking responsibility is where it really all starts. Yet this is one of the hardest things for people to do. It is so easy to point the finger of blame at someone else. I believe that this is the major reason most people never make it to their dream. They simply aren't willing to take responsibility for where they are, who they are, and what they have. They lay blame anywhere but where it belongs.

They blame:

their background
their environment
their parents
their family
their education
their spouse
their job
their boss
their company
the economy
the government
the school system
the weather

They say they are:

too old . . . too young
too fat . . . too skinny

People will blame the strangest things! There are some problems with a list like this. First, most people fail to put the most critical item on the list: **themselves!** Secondly, it does no good to blame. Blame won't fix anything.

Don't fix the blame, fix the problem!

So if you have a list like this, be sure your name is on it, and then throw it away.

Take responsibility for where you are. Take responsibility for who you are. Take responsibility for what you have. You can't take one step on the road to success until you first take responsibility for yourself. Don't bother offering yourself any excuses, none of them are valid. You might say, "Well, you just don't know my circumstances." Your circumstances have **nothing** to do with whether you make it or not. I like what George Bernard Shaw said:

People are always blaming their circumstances for what they are. I don't believe in circumstances. The people who get on in this world are the people who get up and look for the circumstances they want, and, if they can't find them, make them!

So don't go blaming your circumstances, no matter how bad they may seem. I can give you literally thousands of examples of people who have overcome incredible odds and terrible circumstances to achieve outstanding results. And I will make you this guarantee: **none** of them made it until they first took responsibility.

Make a list of items/circumstances you will no longer blame and are ready to take responsibility for:

CHAPTER THREE

Make A Decision

Choice, not chance, determines destiny.

Unknown

Not to decide is to decide.

Harvey Cox

First you make your decisions, then your decisions make you.

Unknown

Choose action, not rest. Choose truth, not fantasy. Choose a smile, not a frown. Choose love, not animosity. Choose the good in life in all things, and choose the opportunity as well as the chance to work when springtime smiles on your life.

Jim Rohn

Always bear in mind that your own resolution to succeed is more important than any other one thing.

Abraham Lincoln

Whenever I make a bum decision, I just go out and make another.

Harry S. Truman

There is a story of a man who is about to take over as president of a manufacturing company. The retiring president was still on duty for a few more days, so the man decided to take advantage of the retiring president's knowledge by asking him his key to success.

The retiring man barked out the answer to the question: "Two words, GOOD DECISIONS!" The new fellow said thank you and started to leave when he turned and asked, "How do I learn to make good decisions?" The man answered, "One word, EXPERIENCE!" Again the new president turned and asked, "How do I get experience?" At this point the older man smiled and said, "Two words, BAD DECISIONS."

All of your decisions cannot be good ones. Some decisions must be bad. But you still have to continue to make decisions.

Billionaire H. L. Hunt was once interviewed and was asked for his philosophy of success. He said if you want to be a success you need to do two things: 1. Make a decision about what you want in life. 2. Make a decision about what you're willing to give up to get it.

I believe it is very important to do the two things H. L. Hunt advised. It is important to know what you want and what you are willing to give up in order to get it. However, I believe that the true significance of his statements is that they both start with making a decision.

What kind of decisions have you made in your life? Have you made a decision about what you want out of life? Have you made a decision about what you are willing to give up in order to get it? Have you made decisions in your past that weren't so good? In fact, have you ever made some decisions that are just plain lousy? Sure you have.

That's okay. Believe me you aren't alone. The good news is that your decisions are in the past. You now get to make new decisions. Maybe a decision to fix the problem created by your last decision. A decision to never do it that way again. A decision to do something totally different.

Whatever you decide on is fine, even if it's wrong. It's better to make a bad decision than no decision. And it's much better to make too many decisions than not enough decisions. Whatever you do, don't be like the person who said, "I used to be indecisive, but now I'm not so sure."

Dr. Wayne Dyer says that where you are and what you are is the sum total of the choices you have made. That's great news! That means that if you aren't happy with where you are and what you are, then you can make some new choices and be different!

It is so wonderful to have the power of choice. The ability to make decisions is our God given right. It is what makes us different from the rest of God's creations.

In his seminars, Jim Rohn, a speaker and success philosopher, asks the question, "How big will a tree grow?" The answer is that a tree will grow to be as big as it can. It will put down as may roots as it can; it will grow as many branches as it can; it will put out as many leaves as it can; and it will produce as much fruit as it possibly can. In fact, everything in nature grows to its maximum potential. That is, everything except for people. Why? Because only people have the ability to choose. Sadly, they can choose to be less than they have the ability to be. However, there is great news in this powerful truth. If people have the ability to choose to be **less** than they can be, they also have the ability to choose to be **all** they can be.

Every journey begins with a decision to go. Your journey of success also begins with a decision to go. Make a decision **right now** to begin your journey toward becoming the best version of you that you can possibly be!

Today I make a decision to be different! I take full responsibility for my life: for who I am, what I am, where I am and what I have. I realize that my future does not in any way have to resemble my past. I am ready to take the first step on my journey to success.

Date ______________________________

Signature __________________________

CHAPTER FOUR

Change

It is only when you exercise your right to choose that you can also exercise your right to change.

Shad Helmstetter

I may not be the man I want to be; I may not be the man I ought to be; I may not be the man I could be; I may not be the man I can be; but praise God, I'm not the man I once was.

Martin Luther King, Jr.

The greatest discovery of my generation is that human beings can alter their lives by altering their attitudes of mind.

William James

The chains of habit are too weak to feel until they are too strong to break.

Unknown

If you are going to change your life, you need to start immediately and you need to do it flamboyantly.

William James

It is amazing how many people want things to be different for them and yet they aren't willing to **do** anything different. I know people who **wish** for things to be different, **wish** they had a better job, and **wish** they were smarter.

Wishing doesn't work. You can wish for things to be different and they'll never change. Wishing for things to be different will not change your circumstances or your results. As Zig Ziglar says, "As long as you keep on doin' what you been doin', then you're going to keep on gettin' what you been gettin'." A simple truth that says so much. If you want to change your "gettin" then you better change your "doin'." In other words, if you want to change your results, you better change your actions.

I have fallen victim to the "Wishing Syndrome" more than once. When things were not as I wanted them in my life, I would **wish** for things to get better. That's when I learned one of the most profound truths of my life:

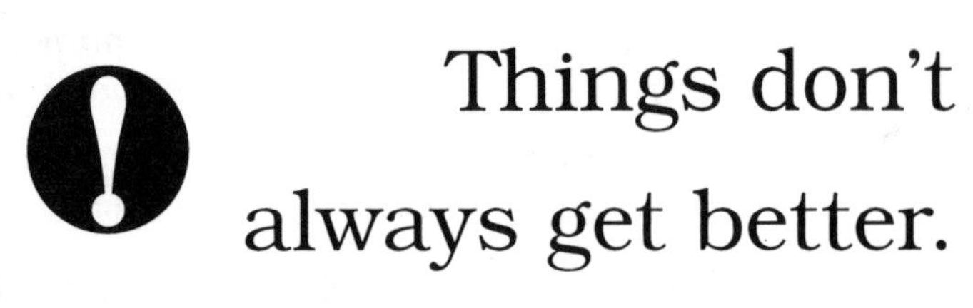

What a statement to make. I bet that you've been told just the opposite.

Statements like:

"Be patient, things will get better."
"Just wait until ___(Fill in the blank.)___ and things will be better."
"Just take this medicine and things will get better."

"Trust me, it'll be okay."
"Things will be better in the morning."
And on . . . and on . . . and on.

My experience just won't validate these statements. In my particular case, things didn't get better, they got worse. Mr. Murphy of Murphy's Law fame came to live with me. He moved into my spare bedroom and ate all my food. But that was good, because it taught me a great lesson. It taught me the real truth in dealing with the fact that things don't always get better. The truth is: since things don't always get better . . .

You have
to get better.

This was great news for me. It put me back in control of my circumstances. Being out of control is scary and dangerous. Having circumstances take over will normally head you toward total annihilation. You must get back in control by changing yourself. You can't keep doing the same thing, you can't keep being the same way, you can't keep dealing with the same people in the same manner, and you can't keep thinking like you have been thinking.

You've got to CHANGE!

Change is your only hope. Otherwise your future will look just like your past. The quotes used at the beginning of this chapter are particularly significant. William James, the father of American psychology, says that you can change your life by changing your attitude. Does your attitude need to be changed? Mine did. When my business failed, I was embarrassed, broke, and defeated. I desperately needed a change in my life. It started with a change in attitude. I had to believe that my life was not over, and that this was only a temporary setback.

When it seems like you've lost everything, you still have something very important left: POTENTIAL. That became my focus. I had nothing left to lose so why not go for it? I started looking at what I had left: my health, my family, my faith, and my abilities. That was the attitude I had to develop for survival and to win. And that required a change.

When should you make your change? William James said to do it **immediately** and to do it **flamboyantly.** Let me propose it to you by using an old sales technique called the Three Question Close.

1. Can you see where making a change would help your life?
2. Are you interested in helping your life?
3. If you were ever going to start helping your life, when would be the best time to start?

The answer is obviously now.

I suggest you use the Three Question Close to create a sense of urgency in any area of your life where you feel you need a change. For instance:

1. Can you see where losing weight would make you healthier?
2. Are you interested in being healthier?
3. If you were ever going to start being healthier, when would be the best time to start?

Again, the answer is now.

Spend some time on this if you are a person who has a tendency to put off change in your life. Fill in the blanks with any change or any benefit you would like to have in your life. Again, write them down. Experiencing them in this way will help you focus more on your desired outcome.

1. Can I see where (the change) would (the benefit) ?
2. Am I interested in (the benefit) ? OR Do I want to be (the benefit)?
3. If I was ever going to start being/doing/or having (the benefit) , when would be the best time to start?

I hope this exercise helps you create a sense of urgency in making changes in your life.

Change is necessary in order for us to grow. And growth is key to success. Unless you are 100% satisfied with who you are, where you are, what you are doing and what you have (and I've never met anyone yet who is), then you are going to have to do some changing to get there. I know change is uncomfortable. It introduces an element of risk. And with risk comes a possibility of failure. Get that out of your mind!

There is no failure as long as you are moving forward.

Let me explain. Failure is a result of not doing. Period. If you do something, then you win. Even if you didn't do it as well as you could have, should have, or will, the point is you did it.

The failure is in not changing. There is no failure in any kind of growth. No matter how small or insignificant it may seem to you at the time, you can only grow to be more, never to be less. Therefore, you always win.

In order to understand the power of change in your life, memorize these words:

> ! If you want something you have never had, you've got to do something you have never done.
>
> **Mike Murdock**

List several changes which you need or want to make in your life and the benefits of making the change.

Change	Benefit

Chapter Five

Be Willing

Impossible is a word to be found in the dictionary of fools.

Napoleon

There are two kinds of men in this world, those who wish and those who will. The world belongs to those who will.

Louis L'Amour

It's not how good a man shoots that matters. What matters is how willing he is to shoot when there's someone shootin' back at him. A lot are good, few are willing.

John Wayne in The Shootist

In Mike Hernacki's book, The Ultimate Secret To Getting Absolutely Everything You Want, he says that in order to accomplish anything, you have to be willing to do whatever it takes to accomplish it. Now that sounds pretty simple. It sounds like something we could all agree with. But look closely at what he said and didn't say. He didn't say that you had to actually **do** whatever it takes to get what you want. He said you had to be **willing** to do whatever it takes in order to get what you want. There is a significant difference. Life will rarely ask you to do whatever it takes. It will, however, ask you to be willing to do whatever it takes.

Are you willing to do whatever it takes? I thought that I was.

I had decided I was going to become a full-time professional speaker. There was just one problem: I wasn't doing enough speaking to pay my bills. But I had made up my mind that I was willing to do **whatever** it took in order to make it. Now I knew I was a good salesman. But when I became a full-time speaker, I became a great salesman. I sold my car first, then my watch, then my furniture. I had dozens of garage sales. I was like the guy who sold everything he owned except for his bicycle and it had no seat and no handlebars. He had lost his rear and didn't know which way to turn

Because I had made the **decision** that I was **willing** to do whatever it takes, I did it. It wasn't easy. But it was worth it. Part of my inspiration during this time came from a poster I have in my office. It is a picture of Thomas Edison with this quote: "Many of life's failures are men who did not realize how close they were to success when they gave up."

I'll ask you again. Are you willing to do whatever it takes? Are you willing to stay as long as it takes? Are you willing face any adversity? Are you willing to pay the price so you can enjoy the benefits?

The world is not made up of the have's and have-not's — but of the will's and will-not's.

I am willing to do whatever it takes in order to get what I want out of life!

____

Signature of commitment

Chapter Six

Have Vision

The vision that you glorify in your mind, the ideal that you enthrone in your heart - this you will build your life by, this you will become.

James Allen

Whatever the mind can conceive and believe it can achieve.

Napoleon Hill

Whatever you vividly imagine, ardently desire, sincerely believe, and enthusiastically act upon must inevitably come to pass.

Paul J. Meyer

The future belongs to those who believe in the beauty of their dreams.

Eleanor Roosevelt

Where there is no vision, the people perish.

Proverbs 29:18

A vision without a task is a dream; a task without a vision is drudgery; a vision and a task is the hope of the world.

Unknown

What kind of vision do you have for your life? Can you visualize the kind of life you want to lead? Can you visualize the kind of work you want to be doing? Can you see yourself as the kind of person you want to be? Can you visualize the kind of home you want to live in, the kind of car you want to drive, the kind of physique you want to have?

After my wife and I had been living in our house for a few years, we talked about how great it would be to have a swimming pool in our backyard. She loves the sun and I love the water, so it seemed like a good idea to plan for a pool. So I went into the backyard, got some wooden stakes and some string and staked out the pool. She thought I was crazy. When I put a board at one end and told her that was the diving board, she **knew** I was crazy. I stopped mowing the grass between the strings. Why? Because that was my swimming pool and you don't mow water, do you? When I put a pool float in that tall grass and sipped a glass of ice tea while floating in my pool, she almost called a psychiatrist. But I knew that was my pool and we would have one in that very spot. I visualized it in my mind and acted upon the visualization.

Rose Mary, the logical one in our house, told me all of the reasons we couldn't/shouldn't have a pool. We couldn't afford it. We had a dog that would probably drown. I would get sunburned (I can burn in the glow of a 100 watt lightbulb). It wouldn't improve our property value all that much. The list seemed endless. I finally worked her through every objection except for the issue of money. That was when we decided to pursue refinancing our house at a better interest rate. We were able to take our adjustable rate mortgage down over four percentage points, finance the pool, and still save nearly $300 per month over our previous house payment!

When the pool company showed up to dig our swimming pool they said, "Where do you want it?" I replied, "Just dig up all that tall grass between those strings!"

You say, "That's not visualization, that's money management." Yes, but we would never have pursued the idea and sought the alternate financing without the visualization of the desired goal of a swimming pool in our back yard. Visualization works!

And it will work in all areas of your life. I firmly believe you have to be able to picture what you want to have if you are ever going to have it. I know you must visualize what you want to be if you are ever going to be it. You must see yourself as having the abilities before you will ever get those abilities. In other words, you must have vision for your life.

I believe we all have vision. It's just not always good, positive vision. I know some people picture in their minds exactly what they **don't** want to have happen. This is called WORRY. Worry is visualizing something negative in advance of it happening. What a waste of time. I have heard it said that worry is simply the misuse of the imagination. I believe that, especially when you realize that over 90% of what people worry about never happens.

Wouldn't it be better to use your ability to visualize in a positive manner? Of course! Start now by picturing in your mind what you want to happen.

Look back at the quote by Napoleon Hill.

Whatever the mind can conceive and believe it can achieve.

The operative word in this statement is WHATEVER. There are no limits on the word WHATEVER. That means that you can create a vision for your life that has no limits, no boundaries. Isn't that exciting? Say YES!

Don't waste another moment of your life creating a picture of what you **don't want.** From this point on, **ONLY** create pictures in your mind of what you **do want.**

Remember this. **You must see it first in your mind if you are ever going to see it in your reality.**

Make a list of your positive visions for your future:

CHAPTER SEVEN

Have Goals

Aim at nothing and you'll probably hit it.

Unknown

You are never going to make it as a wandering generality; you have got to become a meaningful specific.

Zig Ziglar

Make no little plans; they have no magic to stir men's blood and probably themselves will not be realized. Make big plans; aim high in hope and work, remembering that a noble, logical diagram once recorded will not die.

Daniel H. Burnham

You show me a stock clerk with a goal and I'll show you a person who will make history. But you show me a person without a goal and I'll show you a stock clerk.

J. C. Penney

Why is there so much emphasis placed on goal setting? Because it works! Nothing you can do will have any more impact on your future than your goals. Goals are like magnets; they draw you closer to them. So get good at goal setting!

How many people actually **have** goals? Everyone. You had a goal to get up this morning and you probably made it. You had a goal to read this book, and you've made it this far. You have a goal to be around tomorrow. We all have goals. Not always clearly defined, not always well thought out, not always specific or even purposely set, but nevertheless, you have goals.

How many people **set** goals? Very few. Studies indicate that only 3% of our society has written down goals for their life. No wonder people aren't ending up where they want to be.

What is the difference between **having** goals and **setting** goals? The difference is the process you go through. Goal setting is more scientific. It requires thought and planning. It takes time. Let's look at the process of goal setting.

First, make a list of everything that you want to **be**, everything you want to **do**, and everything you want to **have** - the three categories in which you should set goals. This will take you some time. Take all of the time you need. In the goal setting workshops which I conduct around the country I have found something very interesting and very sad. Most adults are hard pressed to come up with more than two or three items in each of these categories. We are hung up on all of the negative programming that tells us everything that we **can't** be, do or have. Think for a moment about asking five year olds to make a list of everything they want to be, and another list of everything that they want to do and a third list of everything that they want to have. Be prepared to give them a **big** stack of paper because they can think of hundreds of things. They haven't been told all of the negatives yet. They haven't bought into the limitations pressed on them by others. They still really believe that they actually can be, do or have all of those things. That's how we should be as adults. So when you make your list, think like a kid again. Don't let time, money, education, background, environment, or anything else act as a limitation on your mind. Look again at the words of Napoleon Hill:

> "Whatever the mind can conceive and believe, it can achieve."

The most important word in this statement is the word **whatever.** There are no limitations on this word. There are no limitations on you either.

So right now, make a list on the pages provided here of everything you want to be, do or have. If you run out of room, and I hope you do, then get more paper. But keep going! Now don't say to yourself, "Oh, I'll just skip this part. After all, I know what I want. I don't need to write it down." Yes you do! **You must write it down.** A goal not written down is a wish. And wishes just don't come true. Goals do!

Remember to Think Big! I have never seen anyone sit down and write out a plan for a mediocre life. But I see lots of people living one. This goal setting process should force you to set some really big goals for your life. That's one of the problems with people who set goals. They set small goals. Don't do that! Set big goals. Goals that will challenge you to be more, and do more, and have more than ever before. Goals that will motivate you to greater things.

If you get hung up along the way, then stop and ask yourself this question:

> **!** What would I attempt if I knew I could not fail?

This should open up your mind so you can start again. Absolutely do not quit until you have at least 25 items on each list. You can have more than this, of course, but don't have any less than this. Sometimes it takes 25 items just to get your mind loose enough to really get started. And don't judge the things that you are writing down - not at this point. Just keep writing. You will have plenty of time to analyze them later. So get started!

Everything I want to **BE:**

Everything I want to **DO:**

Everything I want to **HAVE:**

If you are like most people, you probably found that the "Everything I want to **have**" list was the easiest to fill in. That's because we all think of **wants** in terms of **haves.** The next easiest list is the **do** list. We all understand that if you want to **have** something, you must first **do** something. And this is where most people stop. But this is only half way. The full equation of life says that before you can do, you must first be.

> You have to **be** before you can **do**, and you have to **do** before you can **have.**

This is the way it is and must be. You must first become the kind of person who can do the things that will help you get your goals. That is where it starts. What you get when you achieve your goals is not nearly as important as what you become by achieving your goals.

After you have completed your lists (and I hope that you never really complete your lists as you should always be adding to them), then move to the next step.

Make sure that your goals are specific. In my seminars, I always ask to see the hands of those who have a goal to have more money. I get many hands on this one! I then ask one of the participants to come to the front of the room. I verify that they have a goal of wanting more money. When they say yes, I ask them to hold out their hand and I press a shiny quarter in it. I then immediately congratulate them for having achieved their goal and everyone in the room joins me in a rousing round of applause for the person who has achieved their goal.

The look on their face says it all. That quarter is not what they had in mind at all! They had in mind **much** more than that. However, that's not what they said. They said they wanted **more.** Not **how much more.** Then when they got what they said they wanted it wasn't what they had in mind at all.

That's exactly what so many of us say. We say we want more and aren't specific. Then when we get more, it wasn't what we had in mind.

Want to weigh less? How much less, exactly?

Want a new house? Where? On what street? How many stories does it have? Brick or frame? With a pool? With a big yard?

Want a new car? What color is it? How many doors does it have? What model is it? How much does it cost? What kind of wheels?

Want more money? How much more? A hundred a week? A thousand a month? A million?

I want to spend more time with our family. How much more time? An hour a day? One full day a week?

When you set your goals, make them **verrrrry specific!** "More" is not specific. Amounts are specific. Set goals in terms of amounts: minutes, hours, weeks, months, years, color, size, dollars, numbers, square feet. **Be specific.**

State your goal as an affirmation. I'll spend much more time on affirmations in another chapter. Just be sure to state your goal positively and in the present tense. This is one of the major reasons people don't achieve their goals.

Then make sure that the goal is really YOUR goal. You can't work with true commitment on a goal that isn't yours. You don't really get going on a goal that your boss, or your doctor, or your spouse set for you. For you to get going on the goal, it must be yours.

Make sure that your goals are not in conflict with each other. I had a goal one time to eat a two pound bag of M & M's everyday. And I did it nearly everyday for over six months. At the same time, I had a goal to weigh 165 pounds and have a 34" waist. I found out that you can't do both. My goals were in conflict.

Get emotionally committed to your goals. In the world of selling we know that people buy **emotionally** and justify their purchase **logically.** You will buy into your goal the very same way. I saw a man recently shopping in a store with two small oxygen tubes in his nostrils. He was pushing with one hand a small two-wheeler with an oxygen tank on it. With the other hand he was smoking a cigar. I'll guarantee you that his doctor had set a goal for him to quit smoking. I'll bet you that his family had a goal for him to quit smoking. But there he was, unable to breathe on his own, forced to carry oxygen with him at all times, still smoking.

It was not **his** goal to quit smoking. And even though he **logically** knew that smoking was killing him, he hadn't bought into it **emotionally**.

At this point you are ready to get started. I want to give you a ten step formula for goal achievement. I call it "How To Get What I Want." If you will follow this formula with each of your goals then I'll guarantee you better results than you've had before with no formula.

How To Get What I Want

Step # 1 - Exactly what I want to be, do or have. (written as an affirmation.)

Step # 2 - Why I want it.

Write down all of the reasons that you want your goal. Take your time. There will be many times when things aren't going the way you had in mind and you'll have to come back to this section to remind yourself of the reasons you set this goal to begin with. So do a good job here. If you have a strong enough **why** you can endure any **how**.

Step # 3 - Obstacles I face.

It is important to write down the obstacles that you know you will encounter along the way. It will help you prepare your defense against them. It will also put them in the proper perspective. Obstacles, when written down, get smaller. Caution: Don't whine to yourself in this section. We are **so** good at coming up with hundreds of reasons why we can't, shouldn't, or never will be able to. Forget those things and concentrate on legitimate obstacles that must be dealt with in order to reach your goal.

Step # 4 - What I already know about how to achieve my goal.

We all know something about our goal, otherwise we wouldn't know that it was something we wanted. Write down what you know. Take credit for the knowledge that you already have, and the research you've already done.

Step # 5 - What I need to know.

We all need more information on how to achieve our goals. We either need to know more about the goal, or more about the process by which to reach it, or more about ourselves. If you desire to weigh less, you may need to know more about nutrition or exercise. If you want to be a better parent, you may need to read some books on parenting. In this section write down the additional information you need to acquire.

Step # 6 - The people who can help me reach my goal.

These may include people you are already acquainted with, or even know very well; like your boss, your spouse, your doctor, your minister or a special friend. Or it may include people you haven't met yet but know they could help you achieve your goal. Regardless of the names you write down here, be careful. When you involve someone in your goals, you are laying a little bit of you on the line. Some people will not treat that little bit of you with care. They'll tell you all of the reasons that you shouldn't try it, that it won't work, and that it isn't right for you. Do not walk away from these people; run from these people.

Step # 7 - The PLAN for achieving my goal.

This is the biggy! Take great care with your plan. Tomorrow when you wake up, it won't make any difference how much you love your goal. However, it will make a lot of difference how much you love your plan. Your plan is what you are faced with every minute of every day. Make sure that it is a good one. Make sure that your plan focuses on accomplishment and not activity. Accomplishment orientation forces you to constantly be asking yourself, "What am I getting done?" Activity orientation asks the question, "What am I doing?" See the difference? There is nothing more frustrating than to find out that you are absolutely excellent at doing something that didn't need to be done at all.

Beware of those who tell you not to worry about the plan. Some say, just set the goal and you will be drawn to it and it will be drawn to you. They are exactly right. But that is irresponsible goal setting. I know! I set a goal to be a full-time professional speaker. I wrote it down and believed it. That was a good goal for me and one that I wanted and knew was right for me. However, I owned another business at the time. So my goal of becoming a full-time professional speaker should have included a logical, systematic, profitable removal of myself from that business. Goals are powerful. They will not only draw you to them, sometimes they will drag you kicking and screaming to them. I needed a plan to go along with my goal. I didn't have one. The result? Business failure. Good goal. No plan. Result . . . Disaster!

Start by looking at the list of people who can help you and write out a plan to contact them to ask for their help. Then look at the list of information you need and create an action plan to obtain it. Plan to review the benefits daily. You get the idea...

Set your goal, make it a big one, believe in it, know the obstacles, involve good people, get the information necessary, and **ALWAYS** have a plan!

Step # 7 - The PLAN (continued)

Step # 8 - What I will do TODAY.

Something must be done today. William James said, "If you are going to change your life, you need to start immediately and you need to do it flamboyantly." Find something you can do today that will get you started toward achieving your goal. Even something very small. The Chinese say that the journey of a thousand leagues begins with a single step. Do not procrastinate. Take action. Do something today.

Step # 9 - Completion Date

Set a date to complete your goal. Some goals don't have completion dates because they are ongoing, lifetime goals. For example, if you set a goal to read one hour a day, you probably don't want to ever stop doing that. But at least monitor your progress for thirty days to stay on target. For goals that do have a true completion date, remember this: if you get to the date before you get the goal, then stop and look at the goal. Is it something you really want? Review step two, "Why I Want It." Resell yourself on the benefits of the goal. Then review step seven, "The Plan." Is the plan solid? Does the plan need work?

What happens if you reach the goal before you reach the completion date? Celebrate and move to the next goal.

Step #10 - Celebrate!

Never forget this critical step. Every achievement deserves celebration. However, I do need to caution you. Some folks celebrate in conflict with their goal. If you have achieved a weight loss, then don't celebrate by eating a pie. If you stopped smoking for a week, then don't celebrate with a cigarette. Decide in advance what the celebration will be. Sometimes this extra incentive will help you achieve your goal.

As you set your goals and repeat this ten step process for each of them, I want you to do one more thing. Check your goals for balance. While I will talk more about balance later, I want you to look carefully at your goals to make sure you are setting and achieving goals in all areas of your life.

Life areas:

Mental / Continuing Education
Physical / Health
Spiritual
Career / Business
Social / Civic
Financial
Family

Without balance you can't be truly successful. So evaluate your lists of everything you want to be, do or have and see if the list covers all of the areas mentioned above.

So much more can be said about goal setting. Hopefully this chapter has given you a guide for setting and achieving goals that will make your life fuller and happier. If you would like more information on goal setting there are any number of wonderful books and tapes available from many authors.

Expect The Best

Be Prepared For The Worst

Celebrate It All!

Chapter Eight

Start

If you don't know how to do something - START!

The Self Starter's Credo

He who hesitates is last.

Mae West

Many people spend their entire life indefinitely preparing to live.

Paul Tournier

Don't talk about it - DO IT!

Grant G. Gard

The way to do things is to begin.

Horace Greeley

Even if you are on the right track, you will get run over if you just sit there.

Will Rogers

. . . if one advances confidently in the direction of his dreams and endeavors to live the life which he has imagined, he will meet with success unexpected in common hours.

Henry David Thoreau

Heaven never helps the man who will not act.

Sophocles

Action may not always bring happiness, but there is no happiness without action.

Benjamin Disraeli

After all is said and done, more is said than done.

Unknown

"Unknown" is perhaps one of the most quoted persons of all time, and was so right with that last statement. It seems as if we spend most of our time talking about what we are going to do, what others should do and what absolutely must be done. However, little actually gets done.

Why is that? There are many reasons and I will address a few.

First, I believe people get so caught up in the planning that they get stuck there. They analyze where they are, where they want to go, and how they must get there. All are excellent and necessary steps. However, these people get **Paralysis By Analysis.**

In my opinion, there are basically four types of people:

Ready - Aim - Fire People. These people get ready. They do their analysis, their planning, and they prepare. Then they take aim. They focus on exactly what they want to go after. Then they fire. In other words, they get started. They take action. These people get things done. This is the type of person we should all strive to be.

Ready - Fire - Aim People. The people in this crowd do their planning and preparation but they lack specific focus; there is no aim. But they fire anyway. When the smoke clears they say, "What did I hit?"

Fire - Fire - Fire People. These are the ones with no planning, no preparation, no focus, and no aim. They just start shooting. You'll recognize these people easily. They make a lot of noise and never hit very much. They are like the fellow who runs to the edge of the woods with his gun, points it into the woods and shoots. Then he says, "I hope something good runs into that."

All of us either know people in these categories, or find ourselves in one of them. If not, maybe you fall into the following category, the one I believe is definitely the most dangerous.

Ready . . . Ready . . . Ready . . . Ready . . . Aim - Aim - Aim - Ready . . . What's wrong with this scenario? These people never shoot! They spend all of their time in planning and preparation. They can't hit anything because they never shoot at anything. Paralysis by analysis. These are people **"indefinitely preparing to live."**

These folks have at least a hundred excuses why they need to wait to get started:

They don't know how.
They're waiting for school to get out or for school to start.
They are waiting for the holidays to be over.
. . . for cold weather
. . . for warm weather
. . . for the new year
. . . until the kids are out of school
. . . until retirement
. . . until vacation
. . . until they have more time
. . . until they find a job
. . . until they get all of their ducks in a row.
Until, until, until . . .

I once heard it so eloquently stated: "As long as you are waiting for changes out there to take place before you make changes in yourself, then you are never going to get started."

I know the importance of planning. I am aware that it is better to prepare and take aim than it is to just go off "half-cocked" and start firing. But while I am a big believer in planning, I am a bigger believer in starting.

Secondly, there are those who never start because of fear of what might happen. Fear of failure.

> ! There is no failure in doing. There is only failure in NOT doing.

That's right. There is always success in doing. When you do, you win. Even if you don't do it as well as you **wanted to do it**, or as well as you **could do it**, or as well as you **will do it** next time. The bottom line is, you did it! **Celebrate!**

Isn't that a relief? To know that there is no failure, as long as you do. It is better to do something imperfectly than to do nothing perfectly. **Failure comes only when you don't do.**

A part of this syndrome also says that before you start, you must first be good. That way, when you start there is only success. This kind of thinking comes as a result of the words we heard growing up. “Anything worth doing is worth doing well.” Wrong! Anything worth doing is worth doing poorly until you learn to do it well. You can't expect to do it well the first time. Or even the second or third times. It takes time to do things well. So don't let fear of poor performance keep you from starting.

Remember these words:

> **You don't have to be good to start, but you do have to start to be good.**

The third reason people don't start is that they are afraid of criticism. They are worried about what others will say. I once heard of a sure-fire way to avoid criticism:

> *A guaranteed way to avoid criticism:*
>
> **Say nothing.**
>
> **Do nothing.**
>
> **Be nothing.**

That'll work! Every time. And if the comments from others are that important to you, then try this method. However, don't expect to accomplish very much. Don't expect to win. According to Malcolm Forbes, "If you have no critics, you are likely to have no successes."

Another reason people don't get started is the impact of the past. We have a tendency to look at our past accomplishments and especially our disappointments when it is time to embark on a new venture. We say to ourselves, "It didn't work last time, so why should I try this time?" Or, "Nothing I try ever works, so why bother?" Or the ever popular, "If only I wouldn't expect so much." Or want so much. Or "If only I had done things differently." This negative talk will throw you into neutral and keep you from beginning the trip to a better you. Dr. Robert Schuller says, "Change your **if only's** to **move ahead boldly's.**" Get started!

Procrastination is the death of your new beginning. Lack of action will kill your ability to win. Action is the difference between winning and losing.

I have talked about goals. Setting them won't do anything for you. Acting on them will.

Vision is wonderful. But vision alone won't accomplish anything. You must act on your vision.

Take action now! Movement toward your goals and dreams will create momentum. The more you do, the more you will be able to do.

> "If you're not ready to run with the big dogs, don't get off the porch."
>
> Cowboy

You are ready! Get started!

List the things you will start on today!

CHAPTER NINE

Quit

Quit that!

My Mother

If at first you don't succeed, try, try again . . . then quit, no use being a fool about it!

W. C. Fields

It seems strange to follow the chapter "Start" with the chapter "Quit." However, they go together. Sometimes you can't start something new until you first quit something old. And sometimes it's not that we haven't started, it's just that we've started doing the wrong thing, and we need to quit it.

We hear statements like, "Get Involved!" That's terrific if what we are involving ourselves in is the right thing. However, I would guess that about 90% of the things going on around us are exactly the things we **shouldn't** become involved in. Just look at all the negative things we are exposed to during the course of a normal day. Things like idle gossip at the office; or social settings where most of the conversation is about the negative aspects of other people, our community, or society in general; or business meetings where all of the focus is on the problems rather than the solutions. I'm sure that you can easily add to this list. And based on that, I can assure you that involvement in those things is exactly what you shouldn't do. Lack of involvement is sometimes one of the keys to success.

I quoted earlier, "If you keep on doin' what you been doin', then you're gonna keep on gettin' what you been gettin'." So if you don't like what you been gettin', then **quit** what you've been doin'! Its kind of like the old joke about the man who goes to the doctor and says, "Doc, it hurts when I do this," to which the doctor replies, "Then quit doing that!"

There are things you simply have to quit because they are hurting you. Hurting you physically, mentally, spiritually. Hurting your family, your career, your finances, and your chances for success and happiness. What kinds of things am I talking about? There is really a very simple question to ask yourself about the things you are doing that will help you determine if it's something you should continue doing or something you should quit.

Will this activity move me closer to my goals?

While this may sound simple, I can assure you that it isn't. By asking this question you may find out that you have to quit hanging around some of your friends. You may find out that you have to quit smoking, cussing, drinking, watching meaningless television, reading romance novels, or over-reacting to little disruptions. You may have to quit coffee, staying up as late as you do, getting up as late as you do, playing as much golf as you do, fishing, or any number of things.

"But I enjoy some of those things, why do I have to quit things that I enjoy?" Because those things may stand in the way of you getting what you really want. They may stand in the way of you achieving your goals. Because you may be satisfying yourself with short-term gratification and sacrificing long-term success and happiness.

I believe that we are all a reflection of three things. We are a reflection of what we see, what we hear, and the people we associate with.

> **!** You are a reflection of what you see, what you hear, and the people you associate with.

What You See

Just think of the things that you see in the course of a normal day: magazines, television, movies, books, people, and the list goes on and on. Scientists say that we gather information 87% by sight. Information enters your brain first through your eyes. You gather information at a rate of 70,000 images per second. What you see is very important. It has a major impact on your attitudes, your beliefs and your reactions.

Do an analysis of what you spend your time watching.

Think of the television you watch. Do the programs you expose your mind to support your moral, ethical, spiritual, intellectual and physical values? Do they fill you with positive information that will move you closer to your goals? If the answer is no, then quit watching them.

Sound unfair? You say that you watch some television simply for its entertainment value? Understand this: your subconscious mind is gathering all the information and **using** it regardless of its value. Your subconscious mind makes no judgement. It doesn't care if it's getting good stuff or bad stuff or stupid stuff. It just takes what it gets. And **uses** it.

How about the movies you go to and the videos you rent? The very same principle applies.

Think about what you read. Jim Rohn makes a great statement about this. He says to find out what the poor people are reading and then don't read that.

Good advice. I will give my opinions on reading in another chapter. I have also included a list of suggested reading at the back of this book which I know will help change your life.

By this time I know you understand the idea about guarding the door to your mind. That door is the eyes. Be careful about the things that you spend your time watching. Much research is being conducted on the impact of violence and pornography on the mind. Most studies are concluding that many of the violent acts taking place in our society today are influenced heavily by the viewing of television and movie violence. While this may be seen as an extreme example, the influence of the things you watch can have detrimental effects on your life as well. Be tough on yourself and your viewing habits.

Make a list of the television shows you watch; the magazines you subscribe to; and the types of books you read. Then decide whether they are moving you closer to your goals.

What You Hear

Much of the same applies to what you hear. Unless you are watching television and movies with the sound off, then you are getting negative input through hearing the programs. However, there are other things that you must guard against in this category. For instance, the radio.

The first thing that most people do when they get in their car is tune in their radio to their favorite music station. Periodically, the music is interrupted with news (rarely with good news). We listen to music played over and over and over again. Then before we even realize what has happened we are singing all of the words to the songs.

A great lesson is learned at this point. By listening to anything over and over again, we learn it whether we want to or not. It just happens. Like magic. This is called **spaced repetition.** It is how we learn everything. It is based on the simple principle that what you hear over and over again will become a part of you. Just think of it. If you want to learn something, just listen to it over and over again. What great news! However, if you are listening to the television, the radio, or the news, chances are that you are learning the wrong things. If that is the case, then QUIT! Quit listening to things that tear you down. Quit listening to things that affect your attitude in a negative way. Quit listening to things that teach you that which you don't want to know or need to know. Be more selective. I'll talk more about spaced repetition and quality listening in the chapter, "Be Smarter."

Radio and television are not the only things to guard against listening to. We have to also guard against the words that are said directly to us by others. There is a saying we all heard when we were children: "Sticks and stones may break my bones, but words will never hurt me." Nothing could be farther from the truth. People will get over bruises and the hurt cause by sticks and stones fairly quickly. The pain and damage caused by words can take a lifetime to heal.

We are told:

calm down

keep quiet

don't ask for so much

don't try that

you could never do that

who do you think you are?

you're too fat, too skinny

you're too old, too young

you'll never amount to anything

with your luck . . .

that's never been done before

you're not big enough

it's already been tried before

Have you heard things like this before? The principle of spaced repetition applies here as well. If you have heard these things over and over again, they have become a part of you. They have affected your self-image and your confidence and your visualization of success. If you have people in your life saying these things to you, QUIT listening to them and their damaging words.

Make a list of the types of music you listen to as well as the words you hear from others and decide whether these are moving you closer to your goals.

While the words of others are indeed damaging, the real culprit is someone else. Someone very close to you. In fact, the real culprit is you.

> **!** The most damaging words you will ever hear will come from YOU!

Studies tell us that we speak to others at a rate of approximately 140 words per minute. We speak to ourselves at approximately 900 words per minute. That is what you are doing right now. You are repeating in your mind all of the words that you are reading and then you are making editorial comments to yourself about the material, and one idea triggers another and you think about that idea, and on it goes. That's called self-talk. But here is the real importance of all of this. Psychologists tell us that up to 70% of all self-talk is negative. In other words, you tell yourself all of the things that you can't do, shouldn't try, will never do, aren't good enough to do, at a rate of over 600 words per minute. If there is anything that you need to quit, it's this. Quit talking to yourself that way. Replace that negative self-talk with positive self-talk. Tell yourself all of the things that you can do. Tell yourself that you are a worthwhile person. Tell yourself that you deserve all of the good things that life has to offer. Remember the words of Ethel Waters: "God made you and God don't make no junk!"

Tell yourself these things in the present tense as if they are already yours. That makes it an **affirmation.** An affirmation is a positive statement made in the present tense.

Psychologists tell us that the mind can not work in the future or on a negative. Your mind works in the present tense and only on the dominant thought. So tell yourself what you want to be as if you already are. Create it first in your mind and then you will create it in your reality.

Don't worry. I'm not trying to get to cosmic on you. This advice is sound both psychologically and spiritually. .

William James said:

The greatest discovery of my generation is that human beings can alter their lives by altering their attitudes of mind.

The apostle Paul said in his letter to the Romans:

...be ye transformed by the renewing of your mind ...

And Proverbs 23:7 says:

As a man thinketh in his heart, so i he

A Japanese proverb says:

Sooner or later you act out what you really think.

\nd Gautama Buddha said:

The mind is everything; what you think, you become.

Quit saying bad things to yourself about yourself. Start saying good things to yourself about yourself. I suggest that you make a list of affirmations and read them to yours first thing in the morning and last thing at night. I personally have taken it a step farther. I made a tape of my affirmations in my own voice. I play the tape first thing in the morning when I am waking up. The results have been dramatic. I feel better about myself and feel better physically as well.

Remember, you are a reflection of what you hear. Guard yourself from the negative words others may say to you and those you say to yourself.

s: (I started them, you finish them.)

fic.

I fee... ppy.

I feel healthy.

I like myself.

I enjoy life and all that it has to offer.

I am capable of accomplishing anything I decide to go after.

The People You Associate With

A man is known by the company he avoids.

Unknown

Keep away from people who belittle your ambitions. Small people do that, but the really great people make you feel that you, too, can be great.

Mark Twain

He that walketh with wise men shall be wise.

Proverbs 13:20

Tell me thy company and I will tell thee what thou art.

Cervantes

When a dove begins to associate with crows its feathers remain white but its heart grows black.

German Proverb

If you always live with those who are lame, you will yourself learn to limp.

Latin Proverb

Chance makes our parents, but choice makes our friends.

Delille

This is perhaps the toughest one of all. Think of the people with whom you spend your time. The people you hang around with at work. The friends you socialize with on weekends. Then ask yourself the question. **Do these people move me closer to my goals?** If the answer is no, then QUIT associating with them.

I told you this would be tough. In my life this meant that I had to quit socializing with some very good friends. I analyzed the time we spent together and realized that we spent it talking negatively about others or moaning about our problems. The time was not productive. We didn't dream together, or support each other in the pursuit of better things. My wife Rose Mary and I looked at our time, looked at our goals, looked at ourselves and knew it was time to quit being with those people. It was a tough decision. Tough, because we didn't stop caring about them or loving them as friends. Tough because we had to replace the loss with other friends and finding friends is hard work. Was it worth it? You bet.

There is also a good chance that some of the people you associate with are the very ones we talked about in the last segment who are saying the things that you don't need to hear.

Since you can't really make people stop saying those things to you, then quit being around those people.

Analyze your friendships. Analyze the relationships you have with people at work. Think about the people you associate with at your church. Are these relationships moving you closer to your goals?

In some cases this will also mean limiting some of your contact with certain family members. I promote the love of family. But I also promote mental health. But sometimes the two don't go together. Love your family with all of your heart, but protect your own mental health. Shakespeare said, "To thine own self be true." You can't be good for anyone else if not first good for yourself.

The attitudes of others will rub off on you. **Attitudes are contagious.** And bad attitudes are more contagious than good attitudes. It seems that bad always is more contagious than good. I don't know why but it sure seems to work that way. Bad news travels faster than good news. Disease spreads quicker than health. Here's a good one: Ignorance Is More Contagious Than Intelligence.

When you have made the decision to quit being around negative people, be kind. In some cases, you may even want to explain the reason that you can no longer associate with them. You may be surprised at the response. Some people have no idea they are hurting you or that they are being negative. Sometimes the entire relationship will turn around. If that happens, terrific. You have been the catalyst to help another person. However, if it doesn't happen and they are offended, move on. Don't try to make them happy. You can't make everybody happy. Bill Cosby says, "I don't know the key to success, but the key to failure is to try to please everybody."

Make a list of the people with whom you associate and determine if they are moving you closer to where you want to be.

Conclusion

Your actions are an outgrowth of the kind of person you are. The kind of person you are is determined by what goes into your mind. You are in control of what goes into your mind. Be careful. Stand guard at the door of your mind and your life. Be aware at all times what you are allowing to enter your thoughts. Think about your relationships. Think about your actions.

You have to ask yourself the tough question: Is this activity or is this relationship moving me closer to my goals or farther from my goals?

This is the key:

> No action is neutral.
> No relationship is neutral.
> Everything you do and everyone you know either moves you closer to where you want to be or farther away from where you want to be.

CHAPTER TEN

Live With The Setbacks

The way I see it, if you want the rainbow, you gotta put up with the rain.

Dolly Parton

Every end is a new beginning.

Dr. Robert Schuller

There is no education like adversity.

Disraeli

Adversity introduces a man to himself.

Unknown

Not even rhinoceroses make it to the top of the hill without slipping a few times.

Scott Alexander

Opportunity rarely looks like an opportunity. Often opportunity arrives incognito, disguised as misfortune, defeat, and rejection.

Denis Waitley

Setbacks **will** happen! If you think that they won't, then you are naive. When you plant a flower garden in the spring there is one thing that you can always count on: **weeds.** You didn't want them, you certainly didn't plant them, maybe you even took precautions against them; but they are still there. Life is much the same way. It is full of weeds. But if you want flowers, then you can't let the weeds take over. You have to constantly pull them out. You have to deal with them.

In life, if you want good, you will be faced with setbacks. The good you pursue will be challenged. Always. All good is always challenged. Your marital values will be challenged. Your business ethics will be challenged. Your morals and your religious beliefs will be challenged. You can give up and let the good in your life be taken over, but what kind of life would that be? Defend your values! The good in your life is always worth defending.

Notice I am calling the challenges, adversity and problems **setbacks.** I am **not** calling them **failures.** Remember that failure comes in NOT doing. The people who are progressing never fail. They experience setbacks. The person sitting on the floor never falls down. The person crawling slowly along, rarely falls. The person who walks very carefully through life seldom falls. But the person running toward his or her goal is the person who has the highest likelihood of tripping. That's also the person who gets there the fastest and is able to enjoy the prize.

Don't quote the story of the rabbit and the hare to me. In that story the hare lost sight of the goal. That's certainly not what I'm talking about. That story was not about speed, it was about determination, vision, and focus. If you move quickly and with determination, vision and focus, you'll stumble, but you'll also get there!

Living with the setbacks is also where the power of choice

comes into play. You can choose to let the setbacks defeat you or you can simply recognize them as part of the normal progression toward success. Just because you stumble and fall doesn't mean that you have to stay down. Get back up! Dust yourself off and move on!

Next time you experience a setback, just say a very simple word to yourself. The word is **NEXT.** Mark Victor Hansen says to use this four letter word to handle all rejection. He's right; the word has great power. When a setback happens, say "What do I do NEXT?" By saying this you have moved forward. You have passed where you were and are farther down the road to your success.

And that's where you wanted to be: closer to your victory. Not standing still to wallow in self pity. Not left with only the problem to look at, but on down the road. **Say NEXT!**

Notice that the title of the chapter is "Live With The Setbacks." It isn't "Give In To The Setbacks." Never give in. While you have to recognize them as a normal part of life, you don't have to lay down for them. Choose to fight back. Choose to carry on regardless. Choose to live life to the fullest. Choose to win.

Make a list of the setbacks to which you have given in and are now ready to say "NEXT" to:

CHAPTER ELEVEN

Stay

The big shots are only the little shots who keep on shooting.

Cristopher Morley

When faced with a mountain I will not quit! I will keep on striving until I climb over, find a pass through, tunnel underneath, or simply stay and turn the mountain into a gold mine with God's help!

The Possibility Thinker's Creed
Dr. Robert H. Schuller

I hated every minute of the training. But I said, "Don't quit. Suffer now and live the rest of your life as a champion."

Muhammad Ali

Many of life's failures are men who did not realize how close they were to success when they gave up.

Thomas Edison

Our greatest glory is not in never falling but in rising every time we fall.

Confucius

Failure is the line of least persistence.

Unknown

When you get to the end of your rope, tie a knot and hang on.

Theodore Roosevelt

One of the major reasons people don't make it to their goals is that they experience a setback and then quit. They don't stay and fight it out in order to get past the setback. They don't stay to see how long the problem will last or whether it's really a problem. They give in and give up.

One reason is that some folks honestly don't believe they are going to run into any problems. They believe that having a Positive Mental Attitude and being an optimist means you are no longer a realist and that you are blind to the problems of the world. Therefore, they aren't prepared emotionally, intellectually or physically for what inevitably lies ahead of them.

Scott Peck starts his book, The Road Less Traveled, with three very profound words: **Life is difficult.** This is not negative thinking. It is reality. It is also a warning: BE PREPARED!

How To Be Prepared

1. **Accept that life is difficult.** There will always be weeds in your flower garden. That's just how life is. You can't change it and you don't have to like it, but you do have to accept it.

2. **Identify in advance what the obstacles are.** You did this in the goal setting chapter. Knowing the obstacles in advance and writing them down will lessen their effect on you and will help you keep them in the proper perspective. It will also allow you to attack them with more focus.

3. **Get smarter.** Study what others have done to handle a similar situation. No matter what happens to you there is a very good chance that it has happened to someone else. Find out who these people are. Find out if they have a book or a tape series that can help you get smarter about the problem and how to handle it. Find out if there is a support

group which can educate you and support you during the experience.

Fear comes through ignorance. The more you know about something the less you will fear it and the more prepared you will be to handle it and conquer it.

4. **Write down your options.** And there are ALWAYS options. You may say, "There's just no other way . . ." WRONG! There is always another way. The thing to do is to brainstorm in order to come up with as many options as you possibly can. Then carefully choose the best way for you at that time given the information you have available.

Time changes things. The problem will change and you will change. One of the biggest mistakes we can make is to believe there is only **one right answer.** There are **many!** Get creative. Search out **lots** of answers and options. Write them down. Use them.

5. **Become proactive.** Don't sit back and wait for things to surround you and to attack. Take the offense. The best defense is a good offense. When you are reactive then someone or something else is in control. When you are proactive, you are in control. This is a much more powerful position to operate from.

6. **Get committed.** Commitment to your goal will help you make it as much as any other factor. Commitment is best explained with the story of George Washington crossing the Delaware. The troops were cold, most with frostbite; rations were low; they hadn't seen their families in a very long time and they hadn't been paid as promised. However, before crossing the Delaware to fight the British, George Washington met with them and gave them a very simple order. The order was to cross the river, and then burn the boats. Can you imagine their surprise? Burn the boats? I'll just bet that many of them thought that in the thick of the battle they

might slip down to the shore and get back in one of those boats and go home to get warm and get food and see their families. But George was way ahead of them. He told them to burn the boats. He removed all avenues of retreat. He took control of the options. In fact, they were left with only two options; they could win or they could die. With those as your only options, you get real committed to winning.

That's the level of commitment you need when you attack life. You aren't going to get out of life alive anyway so become totally committed to winning. That level of commitment will change your attitude and your results!

These six principles will help you become more prepared for handling setbacks and tough situations. They will give you the courage to **stay.**

Refuse To Quit

I just talked about options. Success comes from knowing your options, having lots of options, and choosing your options well. However, there is one option which must be eliminated. It is the option of quitting. I recently heard Lou Holtz of Notre Dame say, "Those who win in life are those who refuse to quit."

I like that statement. It gives me courage when I'm tired and feeling my efforts are in vain. It encourages me to keep going no matter what happens until I can see a light at the end of the tunnel. However,

Sometimes the light at the end of the tunnel is a train!

I promised to level with you. I agree with the statement, "Refuse to quit." However, sometimes you have to quit. Confused yet? First I say you have to quit. Then I say you have to stay. Then quit again. It **is** confusing.

I had to deal with this confusion in my own life when my

telecommunications business was in so much trouble. One of the reasons that I held on so long to it even after everyone else had given up and I found myself fighting all alone, was the thought that if I filed bankruptcy to close the business, I was quitting. I remembered the words of Winston Churchill who said, "Never give up. Never, never give up." So I vowed to hang on and make it work. No matter what!

That was a mistake. I sought professional help from a banker, an accountant, a tax specialist, and an attorney. They all said to bury it and move on. But I hung on. I refused to quit. I explored all options and they all stunk, but I hung on anyway. I dug the hole deeper and deeper trying to save my dream. Finally, hanging on paid off. I saw the light at the end of the tunnel. It was a train!

Then I realized what this idea of options really meant. I began to understand that one of my options was to say no to this business that I hadn't enjoyed in a long time, that had become the source of personal financial devastation, in order to say yes to my true calling to become a full-time professional speaker. I quit one thing in order to start something else.

Sound like a rationalization? Remember the discussion about balance in the goal setting chapter? There was no way to achieve balance by hanging on. My goal to save the telecommunications company was in direct conflict with my goals for family, career, and financial success. Therefore, I chose the option to bring balance into my life and set myself free to be the best version of me I could possibly be, using my talents to the good of the most people.

I didn't quit, I started! I started bringing healing to myself emotionally, intellectually, and physically. I started bringing healing to my finances which benefited my creditors and my family. I started bringing healing to others by sharing with them what I had learned as a result of the experience. I didn't lose, I won!

When is it time to quit? When all of your efforts don't move you any closer to resolution. Then it's time to quit. Don't use this line of thinking as an opportunity to give up. This means you have **explored all of your options** and have **taken action on them.** It means that you have asked trusted, qualified people for their help and **professional advice.** It means you have wholeheartedly **given it your best.** It means you have **given it time to work.** If you've done these things to the best of your abilities, and no progress is being made, **then quit.** You aren't giving up. It doesn't mean that you are a bad person. It doesn't mean that you are a quitter. It means you are smart. It means you have done your best, accepted the results, and moved on!

> Stay for all you are worth!
> Always give it your best.
> Explore all options.
> Then give yourself
> permission to let
> go and move on!

Useful ideas I have gained from this chapter:

CHAPTER TWELVE

Love Problems

A life without problems is hopeless.

Thomas Merton

Problems are nothing but wake-up calls for creativity.

Gerard Gschwandtner

Problems are the key to your significance.

Mike Murdock

"Whoa! You've gone too far this time! Now you're telling me that I have to LOVE problems?" You might be saying, "I hate problems! If I didn't have any problems things would be terrific." How naive! You must have problems. Without them you can never be successful or happy.

Problems are your reason for being. Problems keep you employed and determine the amount of your paycheck. Problems determine the friends you have. Problems determine the people you associate with. Problems determine the company you work for. Problems determine your spouse. Problems determine which church you go to. Problems pick your restaurants, your cleaners, and your grocery store. **Without problems you are, have and can do NOTHING!** You must learn to love them.

Let's look at some examples:

A minimum wage employee is paid minimum wage because they solve problems that take a minimum amount of expertise. A four dollars per hour clerk is solving four dollars per hour problems. A four thousand dollars per hour consultant is solving four thousand dollars per hour problems. You are paid in direct proportion to the value of the problem you solve. The conclusion? If you aren't happy with the amount of money you are being paid, then you aren't solving big enough problems.

What do you do? Ask for bigger problems that have a greater value to your employer and prove that you have the ability to solve those problems. Soon, you will be paid more for what you do. I'll guarantee it. If not from that employer, then from another one.

If you don't have the ability to solve bigger problems then you have to go get the ability. Get more education. Get more skills. Then take those skills to the world. Remember: **Value is determined by the number of problems and the size of the problems you solve.**

Why are people unemployed? They aren't solving anyone's problem.

The same rule applies to businesses. Businesses succeed in proportion to the number of problems or the size of the problems they solve.

Think about it. Problem: People want food in a hurry. Food that they can buy and eat on the run. Solution: Fast food restaurants.

Problem: People want to get information from one place to another place very quickly. Solution: Overnight mail service.

Problem: They want it quicker than overnight. Solution: Facsimile machines.

See how it works? That's what I meant when I said that problems picked the restaurant you ate at last, the cleaners you go to and the grocery store where you shop. Each of those places solve a particular problem you have.

And they solve your problem in a unique way. Hungry for something spicy? Then a Mexican food restaurant might be the best solution to your problem. Why not a hamburger place? It doesn't solve your problem of wanting something spicy.

The key to success in business is to find a problem and solve it. Very simple. Yet it works every time. You will never fail in business as long as you are offering solutions to problems.

How about your relationships? You associate with people because they solve a problem for you. They solve your problems of loneliness, or they educate you, or any number of other reasons. Maybe you associate with them because you have a need to solve others' problems and they have a problem. You are a match! The process is reciprocal. I have needs and you have needs and when we have a match then we have found success in the relationship. If you've got the need and I've got nothing to offer then there's no match and no reason for us to be together.

This applies not only to business associates but to close friends and even spouses. Did you ever have a really good friend? One so close that you shared everything with each other? Then over some period of time you just grew apart? Maybe one day, you stopped and said, "I wonder what happened? We were so close and now we never talk or see each other."

The reason that sort of thing happens is that you stopped

solving each others problems. As people progress in life, their problems change. Therefore the solutions must change. In other words, people give you the answers they have until they don't have any more to give and then you go elsewhere for your answers. Sound harsh and cruel to talk about relationships on this level? Well, that's just the way it is. We are a problem/solution-based people and society. That's the way it works. No exceptions. You will attract people to you that solve the problems you need to have solved. You will be attracted to people that have problems that you can solve.

So how do relationships last? By loving that person so much that you are perceptive to their changes, their needs and their problems. By establishing trust and confidence in the relationship so you can ask what their problems are. By growing with them so you will continue to have solutions for each other. By caring enough to want to be a solution for someone else.

See how important problems are? We all need problems. More than that, problems are critical for our very existence. That's why you've got to learn to love them. They are necessary for your growth, your self worth and your survival.

Now please don't misunderstand the focus of this chapter. I am **not** saying to become focused on problems. Anyone can focus on problems. Most people do that. Just listen to what people are saying around you. Everyone seems to be focusing on what's wrong with this and the problem with that. That's not it! I am saying to recognize problems for what they are. Understand your need for them. Learn to love them because of the opportunity they offer. And the opportunity they offer is for each of us to be a solution. That's the focus of this chapter.

Be a solution to the problems of others. Every person should make it their goal to bring solutions to their job and to their relationships. When you are solution-based, success will pursue **you.** Because everyone has problems that they are looking for solutions to. The more solutions you offer, the more success you will have.

There are people out there who will criticize me for my use of the word problem in this chapter. They will say that there are not problems, just opportunities. I disagree. A problem is a problem until you turn it into an opportunity. In order to do that, you must follow the right process. Look at the simple ways to success we've covered up to this point.

Take responsibility for the problem. **Make a decision** to do something about the problem. **Be willing** to make a **change** in yourself or the situation in order to handle the problem. **Have a vision** of the problem being solved. **Set a goal** to solve the problem. **Get started** on solving the problem. **Quit** focusing on the problem and start focusing on the solution. Understand that **setbacks and problems happen to everyone. Stay** with the situation until the problems turn around for you.

When you have done this, then you have an opportunity. Until then you have a problem.

Take advantage of every problem. You have the ability to convert problems to opportunities. Learn from them. Believe that there is good in them. Know that your ability to solve them determines your success.

What problems am I currently solving?

What problems am I capable of solving?

CHAPTER THIRTEEN

Sell

Selling is the transference of enthusiasm from the salesperson to the customer.

Unknown

Selling is leading someone toward a desired outcome.

Norman Vincent Peale

Selling is making a lot of noise trying to get someone else to do what you want them to do.

Unknown

Your ability to succeed is in proportion to your ability to sell.

Dale Carnegie

Nothing happens until something is sold.

Red Motley

Unless you are a professional salesperson, you may be saying that this one doesn't apply to you. That's simply not true. This one applies to everyone. **We are all salespeople.** All of us are constantly selling someone else on seeing it our way, doing it our way, or taking action on our ideas.

Are you married? Then you had to sell yourself to your spouse.

Do you have children? Then you are selling them on doing what you want them to do and what is best for them.

Do you have a job? Then you got it because you sold yourself and your abilities.

See what I mean? We are all salespeople. So don't try to deny it or be ashamed of it. Selling is the proudest of professions. It is also the highest paying profession in existence. But even if you don't do it as a profession, you need to become proficient at it.

Be able to sell yourself. First, sell yourself to yourself and then to others. When I conduct sales training sessions, I always start by talking about the salesperson. Believe in yourself and your abilities. If you don't believe in yourself then you are not going to be able to convince others to believe in you.

Be able to sell your product. To do this, you also have to believe in what you have to offer. If you personally don't believe in what you have to offer, whether it be a product, an idea, a service, or the value that you personally bring to a situation, then don't expect anyone else to believe in it enough to act on it either. Think of it this way. If the situation were reversed, would you be willing to take the desired action if the product (or idea, service, etc.) were presented to you in the same fashion you as the salesperson are presenting it? If no, then get yourself a new product.

How do you sell? There are literally thousands of books and tapes that will educate you in the skills necessary to sell. I suggest you read a few good books on selling and see how you can apply the principles to your life. In the meantime, here are just a few of the basics.

Believe in what you say and do.

Belief in your mission is the primary foundation for success in sales. Believe that what you are offering makes a difference. Believe that others will be better off with it than without it. (The "it" can be your ideas, your product, your service, or anything else you are "selling" to people.) Believe in the benefits that others will receive by having it. Believe in it so much that you are an example of it. If you act like it's good for them, then prove it by having it, or doing it, or being it yourself. **The belief you show is the most convincing action you can take in selling others.**

Be real nice.

This is one of the keys for success in selling. Why is this so important? Because all of the money you are ever going to have is currently in the hands of someone else. With that being the case, I believe that it is excellent advice to be really nice to everyone else. They are more apt to share their money with you if you are nice to them. And the nicer you are, the more they will share.

Do what you say you are going to do.

Don't make promises you can't or don't intend to keep. If you promise to call someone back on Monday, then do it on Monday. Not Tuesday, with an excuse for not doing it on Monday. Be reliable. Be consistent. Be trustworthy.

These three principles, when followed, will benefit you in ways beyond your wildest expectations. There is simply no way to go wrong when following these three basic principles. **Study them, know them, take action on them.**

1. **Believe in what you say and do.**
2. **Be real nice.**
3. **Do what you say you are going to do.**

There are many things that go into becoming a great salesperson. As I suggested earlier, read some of the great books on selling. The truly great ones are timeless. Start with How I Raised Myself From Failure To Success In Selling by Frank Bettger. Then read The Greatest Salesman In The World by Og Mandino. You might even want to read my book, Sales Stuff That Works! These three will get you started and provide you with information that will add to your success regardless of your chosen career.

Useful ideas I have gained from this chapter:

Chapter Fourteen

Ask

Ask, and it shall be given you; seek, and you shall find; knock, and it shall be opened unto you: for everyone that asks receives, and he that seeks finds, and to him that knocks it shall be opened.

Matthew 7: 7-8

Judge a man by his questions rather than by his answers.

Voltaire.

I bargained with life for a penny, and life would pay no more,

However, I begged at evening when I counted my scanty score.

For life is a just employer, it gives you what you ask,

But once you have set the wages, why, you must bear the task.

I worked for a menial's hire, only to learn, dismayed,

That any wage I had asked of life, life would have willingly paid.

Unknown

. . . ye have not because ye ask not.

James 4:2

This is a favorite of mine: **asking.** It's the one that we all say we believe in and yet so few of us practice. I know you have heard the ancient principle, "Ask and you shall __________ ."

I doubt that there is anyone who doesn't know the answer is "receive." If you know the principle, do you believe the principle? Most will say, "Sure, I believe it!" Then have you received everything you want to receive? If the answer is no, maybe the problem is your asking.

Many of us live as though the principle says, "**Gripe** and you shall receive." Do you know people like this? They think if they gripe loud enough and long enough they will get what they want. Then when they don't get it, they gripe some more.

Then there are those that live as though the principle says, "**Deserve** and you shall receive." I used to believe this one. As a salesperson, I would sit in my office and deserve all the business I did not get. I had a great product, a great service, and a great price so I deserved to receive. But that's not what the principle says. The principle says ask.

If you have lived very long in the "deserve and you shall receive" mode then you have probably progressed to the most dangerous mode of all. This mode says, "**Need** and you shall receive." I say this one is the most dangerous because it seems unfair. It seems like if you need it, I mean **really** need it, then you ought to receive it. Well, it doesn't work that way. The principle doesn't say that. The principle says ask.

There is magic in asking. Most of what you get will be because you ask for it. Think about it. As a salesperson, if you want more business you've got to ask more prospects to buy. In fact, studies say that over 60% of all selling situations end with nobody asking anybody to buy anything. This won't work. If you want to sell more, ask more people to buy.

Yet the magic of asking applies to all walks of life. Let me give you a few examples:

Want a better job? Ask for it.

Want a raise? Ask for it.

Want help from someone? Ask for it.

Want a discount? Ask for it.

Want a better education? Ask for it.

Want more business? Ask more people.

Want to know some good books to read? Ask someone.

Want some great business advice? Ask for it.

Want to know someone's opinion? Ask for it.

I'll say it again: there is magic in asking. Don't expect to get it because you want it, deserve it, need it or gripe about it. Don't expect others to read your mind. Don't expect good things to interrupt you. Don't expect to receive without asking. The two can not be separated.

You also have to ask yourself some questions. Ask yourself what you have to offer. Ask yourself how you can do it better. Ask yourself how you can do more of it. The answers to these questions alone can have a marvelous effect.

With asking comes great possibilities. Be ready for all of the possibilities.

You may get a **no**. Don't be alarmed by this. In selling we know that over 60% of all buying decisions are made after the customer has said no four times. So when you get a no, keep asking. One way to cut down on your number of no's is to ask intelligently. You wouldn't think of asking to borrow a million dollars from someone who makes $18.000 a year. That would not be asking intelligently.

Also, learn the different types of questions. Learn about open-ended questions, reflective questions, closed-ended questions, and tie-down questions. Get some of the great sales books which can teach you the art of asking good questions. The better you get at asking questions, the better your chances of getting a yes.

You may get a "**maybe later**." When they say "maybe later" they may actually be saying, "absolutely no way ever," and they just don't have the courage to tell you. However, it may only be a postponement. They may mean that the timing isn't right, and to ask again later. When that happens, then ask again later. You would be amazed at the people who never follow up. They never come back to get a yes by asking again.

You may get a **yes**. Then celebrate! You got what you asked for. When this happens, never forget to say thank you. So many ask and receive; then forget to say thank you. This makes it very hard to ask that person again.

And say thank you even when the answer is no. After all, they listened and gave you an answer. That alone deserves a thank you. Some of my very best customers started out by saying no. I believe that it was how I treated them when they said no that greatly influenced them to eventually say yes.

The principle is simple. **Ask and you shall receive.** The follow-up principle is this:

Ask a little,
get a little.
Ask a lot,
get a lot.

Study the art of asking good questions. Learn the different types of questions. Get a Bible with a concordance and look at all of the references to asking. Read the biographies of great men and women and look for the principle of asking in their lives. Become a master of asking!

Become a
Master
Asker.

List areas in your life where you need to apply the principle of asking.

Chapter Fifteen

Be The Right Kind Of Person

Always do right . . . this will gratify some people and astonish the rest.

Mark Twain

When you sow an action, you reap a habit . . .

When you sow a habit, you reap a character . . .

When you sow a character, you reap a destiny!

Unknown

Reputation is what folks think you are. Personality is what you seem to be. Character is what you really are.

Anonymous

When wealth is lost, nothing is lost.

When health is lost, something is lost.

When character is lost, everything is lost.

Unknown

The kind of person you are is more important than any other one ingredient on your road to success. There are many who think you can do good things and be a bad person and still win. Wrong! While it may appear that person is winning, in the long run he or she will lose. Don't always judge things by their appearance: look at the long-term results. Appearances can be deceiving.

When I was growing up, I had a friend who came from a very musical family. All of his sisters were accomplished pianists. He, however, didn't know one note from the next. He had a favorite song, "Last Date," by Floyd Cramer. He convinced his sisters to teach him this song on the piano. They placed his hands on the keys and taught him exactly what to do. He practiced and practiced and eventually could play "Last Date" almost as well as Floyd Cramer himself. At parties, he would love to sit down at the piano and play his song. The crowds were always astounded at his musical genius. They would beg him to play more. He, of course, would politely decline. Appearances indicated that he was a talented pianist. The truth was he knew one song! Don't be fooled by appearances.

Likewise, don't fool others with your appearance. Really be what you say you are. Practice what you preach. Walk your talk. Only then will you have the personal credibility with yourself and others to become a success.

There have been many studies conducted regarding character and its impact on success. Most of them come to a very similar conclusion. They indicate that approximately 15% of your success on the job and in life is based on your technical skills and abilities. Only 15%. The studies go on to say that approximately 85% of your success is based on the kind of person you are, or your character.

Think about it. A person who can set goals and has the perseverance to achieve them; has a good attitude; knows how to make a decision; is open to change; is enthusiastic; has a healthy self image; never stops learning; has a good sense of humor to keep it all in the proper perspective; has balance and cares about others, is bound to be more successful than a person who isn't able to do those things. As an employer aren't you looking for people with those abilities? As an employee, wouldn't you want your boss to have those abilities? Wouldn't you want your spouse and your children and your other family members to have them? Of course you would! A person like that would make a better employee, boss, spouse, etc., and would be more successful at everything!

Remember these words from the chapter on goals:

> ! You have to **be** before you can **do**, and you have to **do** before you can **have.**

This principle can never be circumvented. It is imperative to understand it and believe it.

Being the right kind of person is more important than all of the skills and technical abilities you can ever accumulate. It is the primary difference between winning and losing.

Write a brief description of the kind of person you really are:

Write a brief description of the kind of person you really want to be:

Chapter Sixteen

Be Smarter

If you feed your mind as often as you feed your stomach, then you'll never have to worry about feeding your stomach or a roof over your head or clothes on your back.

Albert Einstein

The Lord gave you two ends, one for sitting and one for thinking. Your success depends upon which you use, heads you win; tails you lose.

Tim Hansel

It's what you learn after you know it all that counts.

John Wooden

Man's mind once stretched by a new idea, never regains its original dimensions.

Oliver Wendell Holmes

The man who doesn't read good books has no advantage over the man who can't read them.

Mark Twain

Most people would sooner die than think; in fact, they do so.

Bertrand Russell

He who adds not to his learning diminishes it.

The Talmud

The recipe for perpetual ignorance is to be satisfied with your opinions and content with your knowledge.

Elbert Hubbard

The man who graduates today and stops learning tomorrow is uneducated the day after.

Newton D. Baker

No matter how much you know, you need to know more. Things are changing too fast for you to be able to succeed with old information. If you have a high school diploma, look around; most people have high school diplomas. Even if you have a college degree, just look around and you'll see that a college degree has now become standard. Any time your knowledge base becomes standard, your results will become standard. And standard results are **not** what you started out to achieve. You want **above standard** results. That means that you have to obtain above standard knowledge. You also have to act on that knowledge. **Remember: Knowledge is NOT power. Implementation of knowledge is power.** But before you can implement it, you must first have it.

At this point you are probably saying, "Okay! I'm convinced! What do I need to study?" That's the easiest part. Look at your goals. Have you decided that there is something in your life you want to pursue? Then that's one thing you need to study. Do you need a better self-image and a better outlook on life? Then that's another thing you'll want to study. Want to be better at your career? Then study that too. Just decide what skills and talents and characteristics you would like to possess, and then find out all you can about them.

You have heard that experience is the best teacher. That's

true. It is also the most costly and the slowest. There simply isn't enough time to get all of the experience you will need by yourself in order to learn all you need to learn in order to succeed. And experience can cost so much. Not only in terms of money, but in effort. So while experience is definitely the best teacher, you can't rely solely on your own. That's when you turn to other people's experience.

Regardless of what you want to learn or what direction you want to pursue, someone else has probably been there. There is also a very good chance one of those people has written a book about their experiences. That's a book you'll want to read. When someone takes twenty years to find out how to do something and they are willing to share all of that knowledge with you, then by all means take advantage of it.

But there's the problem. Most people won't read the books. Some interesting statistics reveal:

> 58% of our society will never read a non-fiction book after high school.
>
> The average American reads only one book of any kind per year.
>
> Only 14% of our society visits a book store or library per year.
>
> Only 10% of those who buy a book will read past the first chapter.

Mark Twain said: "The man who doesn't read good books has no advantage over the man who can't read them."

I beg you not to be one of those people. Read good books. The number one excuse I hear why people don't read is "there just isn't enough time." I have addressed the issue of time already and will again. There is **always** enough time to do what you want to do, if you want to do it badly enough. If you want to succeed badly enough, then you'll find the time. If you can't find the time, then you'll make the time.

To find and make more time I suggest this exercise. On a sheet of paper, write at the top the time you get up. For instance, write 6:30 if that's when you get up. Then go right down the page in 15 minute increments. 6:30, 6:45, 7:00, 7:15, 7:30, 7:45, etc. Do this until the time you go to bed at night. Make seven of these, one for each day of the week. Then for one week keep track of your time in fifteen minute increments.

Sound like a lot of work? It is. But it's worth it. You'll never again tell yourself you don't have the time to read or the time to do anything else worthwhile. You'll find that you have plenty of time. You just don't spend it very productively. I first did this in 1987 and was appalled at the amount of time I discovered I was wasting. And that was after only three days of keeping track of my time.

By doing this I'll bet you can find at least one hour per day you are wasting. One hour you could spend reading. That's plenty. If you can find more, that's terrific. One hour per day will allow even an average reader to complete one book per week. That's 52 books per year. In ten years you will have read over five hundred books and your competition, the **average** American, will have read only ten books. Who has a better chance of winning?

In 1987, I started reading two books per week. I can't begin to convey to you the difference this has made in my life. Reading over a hundred books per year will expand your mind like nothing else. It will give you ideas and opinions you would never have dreamed existed. I suggest you try it.

I'll warn you, though. After reading a few hundred books you will become a tough audience. You will find out that many are saying the very same things in just a little different way. That's okay. Learn from that. If several authors are telling you something works because it worked for them, there is a very good chance it really does work. Remember the principle of spaced repetition. What you hear over and over again will become a part of you.

If you find your mind wanders after reading the same type of book all of the time, then you have a couple of choices. First, you can adjust your expectations. Don't expect every book to spout forth seeds of brilliance on every page. That's just not fair. Start to read each book by asking yourself, "what one great thing can I learn from this book?" Look for the one great idea. Then be grateful that you found one great idea. Look at the return on investment. You spent a few dollars and a couple of days to find one great idea that might possibly be the idea that turns your life around. That makes it a pretty good deal, doesn't it?

Secondly, when you feel like you are in a reading rut, switch around. Read something different. Read a book of quotations, a great biography, or a high quality fiction book. I personally like to read humorists. Some of my favorites are Erma Bombeck, Lewis Grizzard, Tom Bodett, and Garrison Keillor.

Another great way to learn more and become smarter is to listen to audio tapes. Most good books are now available on audio cassette. Great speakers and teachers and motivators are also available on audio cassette. What a terrific way to learn. You are able to get information in your car when you can't do anything else. Again, most people don't do this. The average person will get in the car and immediately reach for the radio dial and tune in their favorite music. I suggest you use this time to make yourself smarter.

If you put only 12,000 miles per year on your car, you have the same time invested as one full college semester. That 12,000 miles is the equivalent of ten forty-hour work weeks (assuming an overall average speed of 30 mph). One university study says that in your life time you will spend 19,000 hours in your car. That is the equivalent of four Ph.D. programs. Use the time in your car to get smarter.

Make a list of the action steps you will take to become smarter.

Chapter Seventeen

Invest

Spend at least as much time on yourself as you do on your job.

Jim Rohn

If a man empties his purse into his head, no one can take it away from him. An investment in knowledge always pays the best interest.

Benjamin Franklin

Investing falls into two categories: money and time.

When I tell people to buy books and to buy tapes, many of them balk. They say, "That stuff costs a lot of money!" Yes, those things do cost money, but it is important to look at these expenditures not as a cost but as an investment. An investment is spending time or money to bring about a future advantage or benefit.

You say, "Why can't I just check out books from the library or borrow them from someone else?" It is not the same.

You have to be able to mark up a book, underline it, highlight it and make notes in the margins to go back and refer to periodically, just as I suggested you do with this book. Plus, I suggest that you buy the books in hardback and not in paperback. Yes, it requires a larger investment. However, you are psychologically impacted in a more positive way by a hardback book than by a paperback book because in your mind the book will have a higher value. Besides the margins are bigger for you to write in and the book will last longer.

You also need to buy the audio and video tapes of great speakers and trainers. These are available directly from the speakers or by mail order from companies such as Nightingale-Conant or CareerTrack. Your bookstore is also full of many of the best new books on audio cassette. Listening to a tape once will be good for you but you will quickly forget the information. Listening to a tape sixteen times will allow you to retain up to 90% of the message.

Audio tapes are the greatest thing to ever come along because they allow you to learn during what would normally be considered as "dead time." Time like when you are driving, or getting dressed in the morning, or mowing the lawn. By listening to tapes, you will never have wasted moments again. Take advantage of this tool to change your life. I know that listening to audio tapes is the most beneficial thing I ever started to do that put me on the road to better living. And the constant renewal I receive from listening to tapes is the best "upper" I have ever found.

You also need to invest your time, energy and money in attending seminars in order to hear in person some of the great speakers traveling the country. There is nothing quite like hearing great speakers in order to feel the energy and see the passion they have for their message. It is also good to see for yourself that these are real people who have had real experiences much like yours.

But again some people say it all just costs too much. They are much like the fellow who finds a pile of gold by the roadside with a sign that says "FREE" sticking in the ground next to it. The fellow starts loading his car as fast as he can and soon realizes that there is more gold than he can possibly carry away by himself. He decides to telephone his best friend to tell him about the gold and have him get his shovel and come help carry away the gold. His friend, upon hearing the request, replies, "Gee, it all sounds great, but I don't **have** a shovel."

The man can't believe his ears! He tells his friend to go buy one and then come help him. To that his friend says, "Do you know what they are getting for shovels these days?"

I believe there are many people just like this when it comes to investing in the books, tapes and seminars that could make them wealthy beyond their dreams. There is literally a gold mine of information available which can change their life, yet they won't make the investment to get it. What a terrible shame.

In addition to investing money, you must invest your time.

But you say, "I just don't have that much time!" Sure you do. We all have the same amount of time. You have 24 hours just the same as I do, or as your neighbor has, or as any one of the world's millionaires. It's not time that is the problem. It's how we use our time. Most people waste their time doing things that won't move them closer to their goals. They spend major time on minor things. Here are a few of the common timewasters:

• **The Television.** Studies say that the television is on more than seven hours per day in the average American household. I haven't seen very much on television that would help me sell more, be a better father or husband, or a better business person. I am not making a blanket condemnation against television. I like television. I am saying that we must be selective. We just aren't careful enough about what we watch. There are some wonderful programs on television - programs that are intellectually stimulating, educational and informative. However, most television doesn't do any of these things. Robert Orben said, "What bothers me about TV is that it tends to take our minds off our minds." Be **very** discriminating.

The biggest problem with television is that it turns us into spectators. It causes us to go through life like most customers go through stores: just looking. Spectators don't win! Players win. Don't waste your time watching life happen to others on a 21" screen. Go out and live!

• **The Telephone.** When you are in your home, you must be in control of what happens there. That means that you have the right and the responsibility **not** to answer the telephone when it interrupts something important you are doing. Important things like:

talking to your children

talking with your spouse

working on your goals

reading

relaxing

praying

meditating

mealtime

None of these things should be interrupted just to answer the telephone. However, most of us are so conditioned to believing that every ringing telephone must be answered that we wouldn't think of just letting it ring. After all, we might miss something. Ha! I'll just bet that most of the calls you get are solicitation calls anyway. Be honest with yourself and I believe you'll agree that you can do without most of the telephone calls you get. If your calls are really that important then buy an answering machine and turn it on during the times that you are doing the really important things in life. Then you can return the call **at your convenience.**

I also know people who get on the phone and stay on the phone forever! Then they blame the phone! They say things like, "I just can't get off the phone." Or, "They keep me on the phone for hours." Remember your option: you can always hang up. "Wouldn't that be rude?" Not nearly as rude as someone wasting your time, or keeping you from doing something that's really important. Take control of the telephone. You pay the bill. It belongs to you. You own it. Don't let it own you.

> **!** Never let the telephone interrupt meals, baths, playing with your kids, relaxing or making love.

• **The Newspaper.** I have seen people get so wrapped up in the newspaper they spend hours devouring every word of it. I am all for the newspaper, but keep it in the right perspective. First, decide how much time is reasonable for the paper. Let's say fifteen minutes.

Then read only the information that is absolutely critical to your personal well-being. Then only read the newspaper when you can allow time **afterwards**, to replace all of the negative information you picked up with positive information. You should never read the paper first thing in the morning (it sets the mood for your entire day in a negative way), and you should never read the paper last thing before bed (it sets the mood for your sleep time in a negative way). This is the same reason to never make television/radio news the first and last thing you do each day.

You probably think at this point that I am a very uninformed person. I can assure you that is not the case. Believe me, I know about most everything that is going on. I know because people who do read the paper, watch the television and listen to the radio news just can't wait to tell me what they have read, seen and heard.

I agree with Thomas Jefferson who said, "I do not take a single newspaper, nor read one a month, and I feel myself infinitely the happier for it."

While there are many other time wasters, I find these to be the most common.

Invest your time wisely. Invest it in your self-improvement. Invest in your family and your goals and your beliefs. The amount you will invest is so small in comparison to the future you will receive.

Make a list of your timewasters along with solutions/ replacements.

CHAPTER EIGHTEEN

Have Enthusiasm

Rejoice evermore . . .

1 Thessalonians 5:16

Men who never get carried away should be.

Malcolm Forbes.

This is the day which the Lord has made; let us rejoice and be glad in it.

Psalm 118:24

If you aren't fired with enthusiasm, you will be fired with enthusiasm.

Vince Lombardi

Enthusiasm makes the difference.

Dr. Norman Vincent Peale

The worst bankrupt is the man who has lost his enthusiasm. Let a man lose everything in the world but his enthusiasm and he will come through again to success.

H. W. Arnold

Nothing great was ever achieved without enthusiasm.

Ralph Waldo Emerson

Every production of genius must be the production of enthusiasm.

Disraeli

Enthusiasm is the vital element toward the individual success of every man or woman.

Conrad Hilton

A man can succeed at almost anything for which he has unlimited enthusiasm.

Charles Schwab

Enthusiasm is that mysterious something that turns an average person into an outstanding individual.

Dr. Robert H. Schuller

None are so old as those who have outlived enthusiasm.

Henry David Thoreau

Ungawa!

Tarzan

Enthusiasm is a very misunderstood quality. Some perceive it to mean jumping up and down, slapping people on the back, and wearing a forced grin on your face all of the time. That is not my definition of enthusiasm.

Enthusiasm is more like bottled energy. Like a pot of boiling water with the lid on. The pot doesn't have to boil over and spew all over for you to know that the energy is there; you can see it and feel it. The same is true with people. The energy, or enthusiasm, doesn't have to spew all over everyone for people to know its there. It can be seen and felt.

The Benefits Of Enthusiasm

1. You'll feel better. That benefit alone is enough for you to buy into the idea of being enthusiastic. There are many sound scientific and medical reasons for this phenomenon. However, the bottom line is this: thinking enthusiastically and feeling enthusiastic will give you physical energy.

2. You'll be a better problem solver. Karl Menninger, of the Menninger Clinic, once said that **attitudes are more important than facts.** The facts of your problem may look on the surface to be insurmountable. However, your attitude toward the problem more than any other thing is what will carry you through to a solution. Enthusiasm will help you become a more solution-oriented person: an individual who can see beyond the immediate and on to the solution.

3. You'll recognize opportunities. Opportunities abound for the enthusiastic individual. Enthusiasm improves your outlook to the point that your eyesight becomes better.

Not your physical eyesight, but the eyesight with which you view the world. Where some see problems, you'll see opportunities. Enthusiasm will give you the energy and belief so you can seize the opportunity and take advantage of it by acting on it.

4. You'll attract a better group of people. Enthusiasm is like a magnet: it attracts. Become enthusiastic about life and your beliefs and you'll find yourself surrounded by people who feel similarly. You'll begin to feed off of each others' enthusiasm. And when you are surrounded by problem-solving, opportunity-recognizing, energized people there is no end to what can be accomplished.

Enthusiasm carries with it many benefits. These are just a few. I suggest you try it and find out the others for yourself. Want to know how to become more enthusiastic?

Tips For Becoming More Enthusiastic

1. Start every day thinking enthusiastically. The way you begin your morning sets the mood for the entire day. Start your morning with affirmations of enthusiasm, well-being and confidence.

2. Become more sensitive. Become acutely aware of the things going on around you. Look at the wonders in nature you experience every day. Be amazed by your own abilities to drive a car or play the piano or type. Find the beauty in the rain, the fog, and the sunshine. Notice kids playing in the park or a puppy playing with a child. It's the little things that we so often overlook that can bring back enthusiasm in life.

3. Surround yourself with enthusiastic people. Enthusiasm is contagious. Find enthusiastic people and catch it from them.

4. Give your enthusiasm away. Let people see and feel the passion you have for life and for your beliefs. What you give away always comes back to you. Give the enthusiasm you have to others and you'll receive even more in its place.

5. Practice! Practice! Practice! Enthusiasm is like bathing: it doesn't last forever. You must renew your enthusiasm often in order for it become a way of life.

Action steps I will take to become more enthusiastic:

CHAPTER NINETEEN

Smile

An insincere smile is always better than a sincere frown.

Unknown

A smile is the light in the window of your face that tells people that your heart is at home.

Unknown

A smile is a gently curved line that sets a lot of things straight.

Robert A. Schuller

Smile; it don't cost nothing!

Henry L. Winget
(My dad)

My dad said many things to me when I was growing up; however, no statement stands out more in my mind than this one. He was one of those wonderful people who just loved to smile. He was known for his smile. He "twinkled" when he smiled. He thought smiling was something that was good for you and for the people who saw you. Many times I would reply that I just didn't feel like smiling. He would just say, "Smile anyway, then you'll feel like it." How right he was.

He also taught me the practical side of smiling. He was a salesman. He knew that people liked to buy from friendly people. Friendly people wear a smile. Therefore, in order to sell more, you must be perceived as friendly, and to be perceived as friendly, you need to smile. Simple logic that works.

My Dad also knew that it's very difficult to be upset with someone who is smiling at you. He worked in retail all of his life, and in working with the public not all experiences with the customer will be pleasant. Sometimes customers are unhappy with the product, the price, the service, the store or even you. However, no matter how upset the customer may be, the most disarming, powerful tactic you can use to neutralize the situation is a smile.

Here is something else I have noticed in my own life. I like for people to smile at me. Few things make me feel any better than having a friend or even a complete stranger give me a big smile. It makes me feel better about myself, better about life, and better toward them. Pretty much a win-win-win situation, wouldn't you say?

Since I like to be smiled at by others, I wanted to figure out how to make it happen more often. I figured it out! **Smile at them first!**

Smiles are reciprocal. If you give one, there is almost a 100% chance that you'll get one back. What a great deal!

So let's summarize.

Smiles:

Make you feel better about yourself.
Make you feel better about life.
Make you feel better about the situation.
Make you feel better about the other person.

Make the other person feel better about himself or herself.
Make the other person feel better about life.
Make the other person feel better about the situation.
Make the other person feel better about you.
Help neutralize unpleasant situations.
Help you sell more.

Do you want these things? I know I do. My suggestion is that you smile as often as you can. Everybody wins! And as my Dad said, " . . . it don't cost nothing!"

Useful ideas I have gained from this chapter:

CHAPTER TWENTY

Be Yourself

The four cornerstones of character on which the structure of this nation was built are: initiative, imagination, ***individuality*** *and independence.*

Capt. Edward Rickenbacker
(emphasis mine)

At one point in my speaking career I made up my mind that I would be just like Zig Ziglar. Zig was the first professional motivational speaker I had ever been exposed to, and was also the inspiration for my turnaround to a more positive life. Therefore, he became my hero and role model. I told myself that I was going to be the next Zig Ziglar. After a few hundred speeches, I realized that I was **not** going to be the next Zig Ziglar. I just didn't have the same stuff that Zig had.

So I set out to be like Jim Rohn. I would be the next Jim Rohn. A few more speeches and I realized that I was not going to be the next Jim Rohn either. So I decided that I would be like Les Brown, or Mark Victor Hansen, or Lou Heckler, or Brian Tracy. But I quickly found out that I didn't have any of their stuff either.

For a while this was very frustrating to me. I wasn't able to be anybody I wanted to be. I just didn't have their stuff. Then it hit me. Of course I didn't have their stuff. I wasn't them. I didn't have their experiences, their successes, their disappointments.

But they didn't have any of my stuff either. I realized that the world didn't need another Zig, or Jim Rohn, or any of the others. While they are all great speakers and have much to say, what the world really needed was Larry Winget. I am unique. Nobody has had my experiences. Nobody has to say exactly what I have to say. Nobody can contribute exactly what I have to contribute.

The very same applies to you. Maybe you have a mentor, a hero, an idol, a great teacher in your life you are trying to be like. You can't do it. You can't be like them. You can learn from them, you can look for qualities in their life that you would like to develop in yours, but you can't be like them. You have to express your qualities in your unique way. Otherwise, you end up frustrated and disappointed, trying to live up to a standard that can not and should not be met. The only standard that must be lived up to is your own personal best.

In all the world there is nobody exactly like you. Since the beginning of time there has never been anyone exactly like you. And until the end of time nobody will ever be exactly like you. Nobody has your eyes, your face, or your voice. Your personality is as unique as your fingerprints. Your talents and abilities are unique. Sure, some may be better at certain things than you, but none can do it exactly like you.

Each of us is unique. Each of us is special. Recognize it, accept it, and celebrate it.

Make a list of the characteristics, talents, and abilities that are uniquely yours.

Chapter Twenty-one

Lighten Up

Blessed is he who has learned to laugh at himself, for he shall never cease to be entertained.

John Powell

The problem solving journey is not a somber, joyless procession. Instead it is a dance, a parade, something closer to a mardi gras than a forced march.

Tim Hansel

There's a time to wink as well as to see.

Benjamin Franklin

A merry heart doeth good like a medicine . . .

Proverbs 17:22

Sometimes a laugh is the only weapon we have.

Roger Rabbit

You can live on bland food so as to avoid an ulcer; drink no tea or coffee or other stimulants, in the name of health; go to bed early and stay away from night life; avoid all controversial subjects so as never to give offense; mind your own business and avoid involvement in other people's problems; spend money only on necessities and save all you can. You can still break your neck in the bathtub, and it will serve you right.

Eileen Gruder

I have a sign in my office that reads, "The Key To Success Is To Take Your Job Seriously, Not Yourself." This is advice we all need from time to time. So **lighten up!**

One sale more or less won't make or break your career. One business deal more or less won't make or break your business. One more red light on your way home from work isn't really that big of a deal. Someone once said that there are two things we should know in order to lead a successful life. They are: 1) Don't sweat the small stuff, and 2) It's all small stuff. So,

Lighten Up!

This also means that it's important to take the time to recognize some of the wonderful opportunities each of us experience daily.

Rose Mary and I were walking through a shopping mall recently when I glanced over at one of the many benches provided for people to rest on and saw a very small, elderly Oriental man. Sitting next to the man on the bench was a live rabbit dressed in a baseball uniform. What a sight! I had to know more. It's just not everyday you run across a man with a rabbit in a baseball uniform. I walked over to the man to ask him about his friend. His response was, "Where I go, he go." I asked if the rabbit had other outfits in addition to the baseball uniform. He said, "Oh yes, many outfits." I thanked this little man for making my day. And he had indeed made my day. In fact, he has made many days since then. Whenever I think of this experience, I smile.

As I walked away from this man and his rabbit friend, I watched all of the people shopping in the mall walk right past him and not even notice. Literally hundreds of people not taking an instant out of their day, to look at this opportunity to celebrate life. I felt sorry for them.

Look at the words of Lloyd Ogilvie:

Opportunities are never missing, but you can miss opportunities.

Think about the things that have happened to you that have caused you to smile. Maybe a vacation you took with your family, or a walk you took while holding hands with your spouse, or your child's smile.

I have an English Bulldog named Elvis. She is absolutely the ugliest animal on earth. But, I call her my "smile thing." The thought of her face, her wiggle and her snorts, make me smile. What is your "smile thing?" It can be anything that brings a smile to your face. An old joke that makes you laugh, a funny experience you once had, or even your dog.

Surround yourself with things that will remind you to lighten up. You can tell by now that I love quotes. I surround myself with quotes and sayings that not only inspire me to be better, but inspire me to lighten up.

I also have my office full of things that I enjoy and that make me laugh. I have a framed movie poster of the very first Lone Ranger movie, and it's signed by Clayton Moore. (This is also one of my most prized possessions!) I have a picture of a gorilla. I have mind-teasers and little toys on my desk. I also have a mechanical hand for those times when I get especially busy and can use "a hand" around the office. My office is full of things that make me smile. Surround yourself with things that make you smile, and you'll enjoy your day much more.

! He who laughs . . .

lasts. Tim Hansel

Make a list of your "smile things."

CHAPTER TWENTY-TWO

Be Positive

Positive thinking is the key to success in business, education, pro football, anything you can mention.

Ron Jaworski

I'm so positive that I'd go after Moby Dick in a rowboat and take the tartar sauce with me.

Zig Ziglar

With the right attitude, all the problems in the world will not make you a failure. With the wrong attitude, all the help in the world will not make you a success.

Warren Deaton

Any fool can criticize, condemn, and complain - and most do.

Dale Carnegie

It is our attitude at the beginning of a difficult task which, more than anything else, will affect its successful outcome.

William James

Any fact facing us is not as important as our attitude toward it, for that determines our success or failure.

Dr. Norman Vincent Peale

It's not your aptitude but your attitude that determines your altitude.

Jesse Jackson

We hear a lot these days about the importance of a positive attitude. In fact, usually when you mention attitude, some just moan and say "Oh no, not more stuff on attitude." I guess these people have seen the hype that sometimes accompanies some of the speakers who talk about attitude. Or they have had it crammed down their throats by someone they know or are close to. It is true that we confuse a positive attitude and enthusiasm with a forced grin, jumping up and down, and blind optimism. But that's not the kind of positive attitude I am talking about. I'm talking about the kind of attitude that looks for the opportunity in the situation.

I have a positive attitude. I tell people that I am so positive that when I travel I carry a hair dryer. On days when I am feeling particularly optimistic, I even plug it in. Now if you have ever seen me, you would know what a positive person I would have to be to do this. I have been without the majority of my hair since high school. I definitely don't need a hair dryer; just a little Mop-n-Glo and a shine rag and I'm ready to go. However, I recently discovered that being bald is Biblical. In Micah 1:16, the Revised Standard Version says, "Expand your baldness." I did.

While I know that having a positive attitude is good, I am not one of those people who thinks a positive attitude will help you do **anything** better. I do know, however, that having a positive attitude will help you do **everything** better than a negative attitude will.

The most important thing that I can tell you about attitude is that it is a choice. You can choose to be positive or you can choose to be negative. Nobody can force you to be either one. You are totally in control of your attitude.

Attitude is a CHOICE!

While many negative things may happen to you in the course of a day, the way you respond to those things is totally up to you. Now you may say that's fine for someone else, but you have no idea of the problems that I face. Problems? You think you're special because you have problems? We all have problems. As long as you are alive you are going to have problems. Dr. Norman Vincent Peale says the only people without problems are in the cemetery. So don't tell me about your problems. In fact, don't bother telling anyone else either. Eighty percent of those you tell about your problems don't care, and the other twenty percent are glad it's you and not them. Besides that, talking about the problem never fixes it. Talk about the solution. That's when you make progress.

Regardless of the fact that you have problems, and we all do, you have the power to choose your response and your attitude toward the problem. So exercise the power of choice in your favor.

Useful ideas I have gained from this chapter:

Chapter Twenty-three

Relax

Possibly the greatest malaise in our country today is our neurotic compulsion to work ...

William McNamara

Where freedom of play has been lost, the world turns into a desert.

Jurgen Moltmann

...in quietness and confidence shall be your strength ...

Isaiah 30:15

It is better to have loafed and lost than never to have loafed at all.

James Thurber

Man can not live by bread alone, he must have peanut butter!

Unknown

The work ethic with which most of us were raised makes relaxation something that is very hard for many to do. We hear cliches like, "It is better to burn out than fade away," and "It's better to wear out than to rust out." These are cute and do apply periodically for those who have a tendency to become a bit lazy. However, they encourage us to forget the importance of relaxation.

Without a time for rest you will indeed burn out physically, emotionally and intellectually. You can't give-give-give with no take or you will run out of anything to give. You can't work-work-work all of the time either. You must take the time to rest and play.

For me, this has always been very hard. I didn't come with an "off switch." I have always been a doer. I used to brag that I could do more by accident than most people could do on purpose. I have often said that I wish life came with a remote control so I could fast forward through the dull parts. I was always on the go, thinking that rest was a waste of time. I believed that if I wasn't doing something, I was being lazy and unproductive; if I didn't continue to do all that I could do every moment, then I would never get what I wanted out of life. I thought relaxation was only for those who weren't really committed to achievement and to excellence. Rest was for sissies.

No major catastrophe happened to make me change my life. I didn't have a heart attack at 35, or a nervous breakdown. I just came to realize that life is so precious and beautiful that I needed to slow down and enjoy it a little more. I have come to enjoy naps, rainy days with a good book, time spent looking out of the window at the birds, and sitting on the floor with my dog.

The reason people have such a hard time with the art of relaxation is that we don't know how to do it, and we have not been taught that it has value.

I see people who spend their day looking forward to their lunch hour, then run like crazy on their lunch hour and come back to work more exhausted than before they left. This not only cheats their employer, but themselves as well. The reason we have lunch hours in the first place is to feed our body and relax our mind in order to make us productive again in the second half of the day.

Some people spend their time at work planning their time off work. Then when they are off work they spend their time worrying about work. They aren't able to enjoy either activity. I have become like the old man who said, "When I works, I works hard. And when I sits, I sits hard." That's the key. Become good at both and don't let one interfere with the other.

Let me give you some techniques I believe will help you with the art of relaxing.

Focus your mind. Only work on one thing at a time. Try this: lay two objects, for instance, a fork and a pencil on the table in front of you. Now concentrate on both at the same time. You can't do it. You simply can't give your best effort toward thinking about both. You can only concentrate on one at a time. You may be fast and can switch very quickly from one to the other, but you can't do both at once.

Just like with the fork and pencil, you can't concentrate on work and play at the same time either. When you try to, one of them suffers. This is doing an injustice to both. Focus your mind. Give your best to whatever you are doing.

Take mini-vacations. Find five minutes during your day to get quiet, close your eyes and think about something relaxing. Relive your last vacation, or create a vision of a future vacation. Think about something that brings you peace: the mountains, the ocean, or trees. Recite to yourself a poem or a scripture. Sing a song that puts you in a peaceful mood. There are many things you can do to enjoy very short periods of time. Get creative and enjoy those moments of time, regardless of how short they may be.

Practice becoming "brain-dead". This is one of the most relaxing experiences you can ever master. You close your eyes and begin to systematically remove everything from your conscious mind. Start by blocking out all noise; refuse to hear it. Then start removing the things that you are thinking about. Since nature abhors a vacuum, you must have something there to replace what you remove. Replace your busy, loud thoughts with quiet soothing peaceful thoughts. This is an excellent exercise to perform just prior to going to sleep. I know people who have mastered the art of becoming 'brain dead" and I admire them for this skill. They have the ability to completely withdraw from the world and totally relax to the point of sleep even in the most noisy and hectic of surroundings. I encourage you to master this technique.

Discover the value of relaxation. I can never convince you that relaxation has any value. No one could ever convince me. I had to discover it all on my own. Practice the techniques I have listed here. Read books that contain relaxation principles. Experiment. Find the techniques that work best for you.

Useful ideas I have gained from this chapter:

CHAPTER TWENTY-FOUR

Be Healthy

The spirit truly is ready, but the flesh is weak.

Mark 14:38

Sometimes people don't get started because they are truly too weak to get started. Their mind is right; their attitude is right; they are enthusiastic; they believe; but they just don't physically have the energy to get going. Their body has fallen victim to too much inactivity. As my dad used to say, "their get-up-and-go has got-up-and-went!"

You might again say that there isn't time. If you don't get healthy, **you won't have any time!**

You might say "I'm too tired to exercise." That's exactly the reason you ought to do it. Exercise gives you energy. I know it sounds crazy and I didn't believe it either until I tried it. It works.

You might say, "I can't afford to go to a spa." Exercise is one of the few things you can do for free. It doesn't cost a dime to go for a walk. Expense can never be an excuse for an unhealthy body.

You might also say, "I don't know exactly what I ought to do to get started." I'm certainly not going to tell you what you should do to get in shape. Go to a doctor. (Make sure it's a healthy doctor. If the doctor you choose smokes, or is overweight, or prescribes pills for you to lose weight, then run, don't walk, to another doctor! You want a doctor who practices what he or she preaches.) Get a complete physical. Ask for an exercise program appropriate for your current condition. Then get started. It would be a shame to have the rest of your life going at peak performance and not live long enough or well enough to enjoy it.

To be rich
and sick
is stupid.

Tom Hopkins

Make a list of the action steps you will make to become healthier.

Chapter Twenty-Five

Keep It In The Right Perspective

Folks are about as happy as they make up their minds to be.

Abraham Lincoln

To me, every hour of light and dark is a miracle, every inch of space is a miracle.

Walt Whitman

The essence of genius is knowing what to overlook.

William James

The dictionary defines perspective as an overview, broad view, comprehensive point of view, viewpoint, or sense of proportion. In other words, scope up and get the big picture.

I used to hear my grandmother say, "What difference does it make, in a hundred years we'll all be dead and gone." I didn't understand that statement for many years. What she was really saying was to scope up and keep life in the right perspective. Let some of the things that upset you and seem so important right now, slide. Ask yourself, "Will this really matter in a month? In a week? In a day? In an hour?"

Look beyond the moment at the big picture. You can not drive a car safely by looking at the road immediately in front of the car. You have to look down the road ahead of you and to the side, and in the rear view mirror in order to make progress in a swift and safe manner. You have to get a bigger perspective. The same is true of life.

I believe one of the major problems with relationships today is that we get things out of perspective. We assign major significance to minor things. Some people blow up at their spouse because the lid was left off of the toothpaste. They say things that hurt the others feelings and damage the relationship. Come on. Does it really matter? No. The incident lost perspective.

When you lose perspective, you fall into the trap of pettiness. Everything becomes a big deal. You become petty about the faults of your friends, your spouse, your kids, yourself, and complete strangers. You make yourself and everyone else completely miserable. You get picky and start to nag.

> **Scope up! Put it in perspective!**

When Rose Mary and I got married we made a vow not to let pettiness creep into our relationship. I believe that we've done a good job of keeping our word. It hasn't always been easy, though. We all have a tendency to get petty from time to time. I know I do. What I have to remind myself of is that I married my wife because I love her. Because she makes me feel special. Because she is unique and different from anyone else in the world. I did not marry her because she always put things away just where I want them or because she can always tell me where I put my car keys.

I see so many relationships in trouble because they have forgotten the reason for the relationship. They lost their broad view, their sense of proportion, their **perspective**.

We must also make sure that we keep our professional life in perspective. Will it matter in fifty years whether you've been a great salesperson? Or attorney? Or manager? Or will it matter more that you've been a great father or mother? Is it more important to have made a lot of money or to have been a great friend? You have to ask yourself questions like these in order to determine the proper perspective for your life.

One of the things I have done to help keep it all in the right perspective is establish symbols in my life. I surround myself with visual images that remind me to keep the right perspective.

On my bathroom mirror is Psalm 118:24: "This is the day that the Lord has made, I will rejoice and be glad in it." This reminds me that I need to say thank you to God for this day and for being alive and able to make the most of it. It also reminds me to be glad of the opportunities that the day holds for me.

In my office, I have a collection of photographs of my family; my wife, my boys, and my dogs. The pictures remind me of what is really important in my life.

I also have a collection of eagles: small statues and pictures. They remind me that you can't soar like an eagle if you're scratching with the turkeys. They remind me of one my favorite inspirational scriptures: "But those who wait on the Lord shall renew their strength. They shall mount up with wings like eagles. They shall run and not be weary, they shall walk and not faint." (Isaiah 40:31)

As I have already mentioned, I also have toys and games and funny things in my office. These remind me to lighten up and not take myself so seriously.

My most significant symbol, however, is the exclamation point. I wear one as a lapel pin. I heard Denis Waitley say one time that we enter life as a question mark and leave it as a period. I liked that idea and decided that if I was going to be a punctuation mark, it would be an exclamation point. Live every day as if you were an exclamation point. Life is just too short not to enjoy every moment of it.

So scope up. Remember the real reason you are here. Focus on the real reason for your relationships. Leave pettiness, pickiness and nagging to someone else. Ask yourself, "Does it really matter?" Establish some symbols. Keep it in the right perspective.

Useful ideas I have gained from this chapter:

CHAPTER TWENTY-SIX

Go Big Or Stay Home

Go Big Or Stay Home.

Larry H. Winget

Life is too short to be little.

Disraeli

To live is the rarest thing in the world - most people exist -that is all.

Oscar Wilde

Fortune favors the bold.

Virgil

For years I have had a sign in my office with these words on it: **Go Big Or Stay Home.** For me, it captures the essence of success. It addresses life style. It goes far beyond, "anything worth doing is worth doing right" and "put your best foot forward" or "give it your best." Go Big Or Stay Home means doing it with style! With flair! With uniqueness!

I have a friend who drives a red Porsche convertible. Along with other members of the local Porsche club, he agreed to drive it in a small town parade near our city. Part way through the parade, he made a decision that this was not the way he wanted to spend his Saturday afternoon. The problem was breaking rank on Main Street of this small town sandwiched between the horses and clowns. However, my friend would never let anything like a few horses and clowns stand between him and freedom.

He pulled to the side, put his Porsche in reverse and drove through the entire portion of the parade that was following him, **backwards**. He even got his picture in the local paper for doing it. The moral of the story: If you are going to go through life backwards, do it in a red Porsche convertible.

The reason I believe that many don't Go Big Or Stay Home is that they make money a condition of living a Go-Big-Or-Stay-Home-Life-Style. This is not necessary. You don't have to have money to go first class. Walk through an airplane and look at the people seated in first class. It won't take you long to see that some of those people are not living a first class life style. They have lost the thrill, the flair, the pizazz!

My parents were of moderate means. Yet they were able to squeeze more life out of a few dollars than most millionaires can. Life for them was an adventure. It wasn't **what** they had, it was how they **enjoyed** what they had.

I wear glasses. I **like** to wear glasses. Even if I could see perfectly, I would probably wear glasses. Glasses break my face into two parts. If I didn't wear glasses, my face would start at my chin and go all the way to the back of my shirt collar. I would look like a big thumb! I have chosen to make glasses fun. Accordingly, I currently have eleven pairs of glasses: blue, red, green, brown, tortoise, clear, purple, one pair that is a combination of colors, jade and purple marbled, and black with white polka dots, and more. They have become somewhat of a trademark for me. They also allow me to live out a Go-Big-Or-Stay-Home-Life-Style. For most people wearing glasses is ordinary and mundane.

Chapter Twenty-seven

Believe

If you can believe, all things are possible to him that believes.

Mark 9:23

He who believes is strong; he who doubts is weak. Strong convictions precede great actions.

J. F. Clarke

Faith is a most precious commodity, without which we should be very badly off.

Sir William Osler

We are twice armed if we fight with faith.

Plato

Believing: this is a touchy one. Normally people immediately associate believing with something religious. And religion is personal so they don't want anyone to mention it to them or to talk to them about it. I can appreciate this position and I will tell you that it is not my intention to preach to anyone. In fact I am going to save the religious side of believing until later.

What is believing? Believing is not merely acceptance. Believing involves action. It is stepping out in the faith that what you believe in, really exists. Some say, "I'll believe it when I see it." That's not believing. That's not walking by faith. That's walking by sight. Others say, "I'll see it when I believe it." That's believing. That's faith. That's taking action on the unseen in order to make it seen.

So what should a person really believe in?

Believe in what is right.

Whatever things are true, whatever things are honest, whatever things are just, whatever things are pure, whatever things are lovely, whatever things are of good report, if there be any virtue, and if there be any praise, think on these things.

Phillipians 4:8

Opinion alters, manner changes, creeds rise and fall, but the moral law is written on the tables of eternity.

Lord Acton

Believe in morality, integrity, honesty, justice, and the truth. Believe in marriage, the institution of the family, in democracy and all that it stands for.

Believe in yourself.

They conquer who believe they can.

Ralph Waldo Emerson.

Whether you think you can or think you can't - you're right.

Henry Ford

It's not what you are that holds you back, it's what you think you're not.

Dr. Denis Waitley

You cannot perform in a manner that is inconsistent with your own self image.

William James

How you feel about yourself will impact your chance at success more than any other thing. It is imperative that you know you are capable and worthwhile. No matter what has happened to you or what you have done, you must believe in yourself and look forward. You have all of the ingredients for success. You have the same ingredients and the same characteristics present in the most successful person who has ever lived.

Do yourself a favor. Make a list right now of all of the qualities you believe a successful person has. Your list will surely include things like perseverance, hard work, and honesty. You have those qualities. I guarantee you have stuck with something even when it wasn't easy, until you finished it; that's perseverance. I'll bet you've worked hard at something too. And I will never be convinced that even the worst of people hasn't done at least one honest thing. See what I mean? Regardless of what shows up on your list, you have those things present in you right now. The quantity may not be what you want it to be. That's okay. You can work on quantity. The bottom line is that the quality is there. All of the qualities for success are present in you right now!

Knowing that you already have all of the qualities you will ever need to succeed is an excellent reason for believing in yourself.

Believe in what you do.

I have found that if I have faith in myself and in the idea I am tinkering with, I usually win out.

Charles F. Kettering

In my sales training seminars, I tell salespeople at the outset that if they don't believe in their product or the company they work for, then they will never be able to convince anyone else to. Belief in what you sell, the company you represent and the service you provide is the foundation of your ability to sell. I go so far as to recommend if you don't feel that way about your product, company or service it is time, right then, to make a change. Otherwise you are cheating yourself, your company and your customer.

I have seen many salespeople succeed with an inferior product and a high price, ALL because they believed totally in their product. Competition never mattered. The price didn't mattered. It was their belief in their product that made the sale.

Whether you are in sales or not (and I've already said that I think we are all salespeople), belief in what you do will determine your success.

You can be a mail clerk or a doctor, a typist or a military general; it doesn't matter. You must believe you are contributing to a greater cause, whether it be to your company's profits or to the satisfaction of your boss, your co-workers or your customers. Believing in what you do is a must if you are ever going to be successful at it.

Believe in other people.

Man travels hundreds of miles to gaze at the broad expanse of the ocean, he looks into the heavens with amazement... he gazes at the rivers and fields and streams in awe, and then passes himself by without a thought... the most amazing creation of all.

St. Augustine (Paraphrased)

None of us can do it alone. We always need others. In my sales training seminars, I tell attendees that all of the money they will ever have is currently in the hands of someone else. And there are only a few ways to get it. Be really nice to them and provide a service worthy of them sharing it with you.

The same principle is true for you, regardless of your profession. Your success depends upon others! Now you might respond with, "But people are so corrupt." True, some are corrupt. People will disappoint you. Not everybody is going to act or respond the way you want them to. That's just the way it is; that's the way people are. Do you want to gripe about it or accept it and move on? I suggest you accept it and move on. In fact, I have some steps to help you in dealing with others.

Accept people the way they are. You don't have to approve or disapprove. Just accept. Don't bother judging. It will only frustrate **you** and alienate **them.**

Respect others' ideas, beliefs, and opinions. Again, don't bother approving or disapproving. Respect that everyone has the right to have their own ideas and to express them, even if they are different from yours, and even if they are wrong.

Enjoy the differences in people. Be amazed that everyone is unique. Look for that uniqueness and then enjoy it. Besides, if everyone were just like you, think how boring it would be. I like the saying, "When two people think just alike, one of them is no longer necessary." Since no two people think just alike, everyone is necessary.

Expect the best from everyone. I have found that you usually get what you expect. I also have learned that people will either live up to or down to your expectations. If you go into any situation expecting to be treated poorly there is a very good chance that's how you will be treated. If you want the best, expect the best.

These four steps will help you in your dealings with others. Practice them and you'll find it's easier to believe in other people.

Believe in the future.

Faith is to believe what we do not see; and the reward of this faith is to see what we believe.

St. Augustine

Your future holds wonderful possibilities, regardless of your past. Believe in those possibilities. Opportunities abound. Most of what people can be in twenty years from a career standpoint, doesn't even exist today. The future is an exciting opportunity that is a result of your present action and belief. You are in control. Remember the saying, "The best way to predict the future is to create it."

Believe in God.

The person who has a firm trust in the Supreme Being is powerful in his power, wise by his wisdom, happy by his happiness.

Joseph Addison

Without divine assistance I can not succeed; with it I can not fail.

Abraham Lincoln

This is very personal, I know. So let me just tell you how I feel personally. I believe in God. In my life, I have believed in many things. I have trusted many things. I have trusted many people. I have always been disappointed. I can truly say that the only thing that I have ever believed in that did not disappoint me, was God. That's all the proof I need to continue believing. Try it. If I'm right, you've gained everything. If I'm wrong, you've lost nothing.

Make a list of the things you believe in:

Chapter Twenty-eight

Care

One thing I know; the only ones among you who will be really happy are those who will have sought and found how to serve.

Albert Schweitzer

Unless life is lived for others, it is not worthwhile.

Mother Teresa

Happiness may be had only by helping others to find it.

Napoleon Hill

The more you help others, the greater your own success will be.

A. L. Williams

No one will care how much you know until they know how much you care.

Gerhard Gschwandtner

The measure of man is in the number of people whom he serves.

Paul D. Moody

No one is useless in this world who lightens the burdens of another.

Charles Dickens

Caring for and about others has a profound impact on your personal and professional success. A lesson I have learned in both areas of life is that when you care more about others than you care about yourself, you'll never have to be concerned about caring for yourself.

> When you care more about others than you care about yourself, you'll never have to be concerned about caring for yourself.

How can you demonstrate caring? Through giving, through service, and through encouragement. I will deal with giving in the next chapter; I will focus here on service and encouragement.

Caring Through Service

Service is a major problem in business. We most often think of it in terms of customer service, but I believe that it is much bigger than that. It is service in general that is slipping.

Let's think of those in our life we provide service to.

In business the list includes, of course, the customer. But it also includes subordinates, supervisors, co-workers, vendors and suppliers. Had you thought of those? As a manager, you must serve your subordinates through perks, working conditions, facilities, money, support, training and leadership. As an employee, you must serve your manager by providing your labor and a cooperative attitude. Can you see the implications of providing excellent service as opposed to poor service?

Look at it on a personal basis. As an individual you must serve your family, specifically your parents, your children, and your spouse. You also provide service to your community, your friends, your government, the organizations and associations you are involved in and your church.

With these opportunities for service in mind, consider this statement by Earl Nightingale:

"Your rewards in life are in direct proportion to your service."

How rewarding are your relationships, both personally and professionally? What is the quality of your service?

My wife Rose Mary and I were recently in New Orleans, one of our favorite places to visit. In the French Quarter we were shopping in one of the many gift shops. We had made our selections and placed them on the counter to pay. The lady owned the shop was wonderfully polite and helpful and made the experience a true delight. After paying, she said that she wanted to give us something. So she presented us with a small handmade doll. I was astounded. I asked why she was doing that. She explained that it was a Cajun custom. It was **lagniappe.** Lagniappe is a Cajun word that means to give someone everything that they expect from the relationship, **and then some.** It is a surprise, a bonus, an extra, something that you did not expect. It was her way of saying thank you for doing business with her.

I have thought about that occasion several times and have told the story to many people. While Rose Mary and I got a nice gift and had a good experience, I know that nice woman also won. She felt good about her gift, and we told others to shop there so it was a good investment in future business on her part. Lagniappe is good for everyone.

Make a list of your professional and personal contacts and write down ways you can provide lagniappe.

Caring Through Encouragement

I watched Dr. Robert Schuller one day on his television program, "The Hour Of Power." He said that if he could only put one word on his tombstone, it would be **"ENCOURAGER."** What a terrific epitaph.

Discourage means to "take courage out of." Encourage means "to put courage into." Think of all the fears people have. Think of the impact you can have on people and their fears by "putting courage into" them. What a goal! What a gift! What a service!

Ways To Encourage Others

Smile. I have already addressed the importance of smiling in an earlier chapter. Practice smiling. It is a powerful act of encouragement.

Say thank you. Surveys say that what people want most from their job is recognition for a job well done. Become a part of making this happen. Say thank you for the service you receive. You will be amazed by the results it will have. Sometimes those simple words will absolutely make another's day.

Write a note of appreciation. While this takes more time than the others, it also has the biggest impact. There is something magic about putting your appreciation in writing. When people read it, the sentiment grows. Their self-esteem improves.

Notes of appreciation can be very simple. In my Sunday School Class, The Encouragers, we use Encouragers' Cards. They are custom made postcards with an encouraging quote on one side, with the other side blank for writing and addressing. We use them not only to encourage other class members but to send to anyone we find could use a word of encouragement or acknowledgement. The investment was so little, yet both the sender and receiver benefit profoundly.

I encourage you to use notes of appreciation in your business as well. Write a brief specific note to a co-worker, subordinate, supervisor, or department for a job well done. Write a note of appreciation to your suppliers for getting something to you on time or for being especially considerate when you last talked, or for anything you can think of that's good. Write a note to your customers telling them how much you appreciate their business. It will not only surprise them, it will create a relationship that all the advertising and money in the world can't buy.

Write a note of appreciation to members of your family. Nothing is more satisfying than knowing all of those routine things we do around the house are noticed and appreciated. It somehow makes doing them worthwhile. Write your spouse a note for looking so nice all of the time, or for bringing you a cup of coffee while you are getting ready in the morning, or for mowing the lawn or picking up the dry cleaning. Write your kids a note for cleaning up their room, or for being good when you were shopping, or for brushing their teeth without being told. We use appreciation notes in my house and we all love to get them. Before my boys were old enough to read they would have us read the notes to them over and over again. I have also discovered that they never throw them away. Both boys keep these notes in a little box in their room. They look at them from time to time and remind me when they haven't gotten one for a while.

Everyone loves to be noticed and to know they aren't being taken for granted. Write them a note to tell them.

Recognize the little things. Notice the things that most people don't notice. Anyone can recognize something big, something obvious. But it takes someone special to notice the details. Look for the details, the little things. Then compliment them. You'll be amazed at the results.

Make a list of things others do for you that you really appreciate. Then write the person a note of appreciation.

Chapter Twenty-nine

Give

You give but little when you give your possessions, it is when you give of yourself that you truly give.

Kahlil Gibran

It is more blessed to give than to receive.

Acts 20:35

The grave of Christopher Chapman in Westminster Abbey, bearing the date 1680, says:

What I gave, I have,
What I spent, I had,
What I left, I lost
By not giving it.

Earn all you can, save all you can, give all you can.

John Wesley

This one was the hardest for me. When getting started on my road to success, I thought that I just didn't have anything to give. This is wrong thinking. We all have something to give.

When I say that, most people start to agree and say, "You're right, I can give my time or some of my old clothes or stuff I'm not using . . . " All of those things are important to give, and I certainly suggest that you give what you can in all of those areas, but that's not all that I'm talking about. I'm talking about MONEY.

Why money? Because it is the thing that most of us take so much time trying to get, trying to keep, and trying to spend, that it holds a very significant position in our lives. Because of its significance, it is usually one of the last things we want to part with, probably because of our conditioning that when we do part with it we want something tangible for it. For instance, when we give a retail store $20, we know we are going to get $20 worth of merchandise for it. When you give your money for the sake of giving, you don't get any merchandise for it. You may not even get a thank you, but you've still got to give it.

Why? There are many reasons.

If you believe in the Bible and in God, you are very clearly told to do so.

And even if you don't believe, then:

You will enjoy the act of giving. When you give someone a bouquet of flowers, who gets to smell them first? You do! You get to enjoy that which you give away. The same principle works with money. When you **give** it away, you will **receive** enjoyment from it.

The principle of giving is reciprocal.

Give and it shall be given unto you; good measure, pressed down, and shaken together, and running over, shall men give into your bosom. For with the same measure that you measure, with it shall be measured to you again.

St. Luke 6:38

Let me share with you an incredible demonstration of the power of giving in my own life. After my business failure, I was broke. So broke I couldn't even pay attention. And because of that, I immediately got out of the habit of giving. Probably a response that most people would forgive. However, as forgiveable as it may have been, it still wasn't right. This "no giving" attitude/excuse I had developed became a habit and continued even after I started having success in my speaking career.

While one of the principles I was speaking on was the "Law of Sowing and Reaping," I just couldn't seem to bring myself to give up any of my money. It had taken too long and was too much of a struggle to give away any of what I had accumulated.

One day as I sat in my office, I had an absolutely overwhelming desire to break this habit and give some money to my church. The amount I felt compelled to give was $100. While that isn't a lot of money, at the time it seemed a huge amount, especially since it was $100 more than I had given in a good long while. Plus, it seemed that I just had so many bills and obligations and Christmas was coming and I needed to spend my money on so many other things. (Probably all excuses you've used before too, right?) Well, I followed my "feeling" and immediately wrote out the check for $100, stuck it in an envelope, addressed it, and put a stamp on it.

I was so afraid I would back out on sending it that I got in my car and took it immediately to the post office. I felt great about doing it. I just knew it was the right thing to do. That night at my home, my doorbell rang. It was my attorney. Since most attorneys don't make house calls, I wondered what in the world he wanted. I invited him in and he told me he that day had a large debt forgiven him, and he wanted to pass on his good fortune by forgiving one of his debtors. So he had stopped by my house to tell me personally that he was forgiving the balance on my account. The balance on my account was **One Hundred Dollars!**

I know many people would say, "That's odd; what an interesting coincidence." I will never be convinced of that. That event forever changed my attitude about giving. That wasn't odd; it was God!

Give! Besides being the right thing to do, it will bring you enjoyment, happiness, and returns like you just won't believe.

Make a list of the ways you currently give and search for ways to increase it.

CHAPTER THIRTY

Know The Law

You can have everything in life you want if you will just help enough other people get what they want.

Zig Ziglar

Your rewards in life are in direct proportion to your service.

Earl Nightingale

For every action there is an equal and opposite reaction.

The Law Of Cause And Effect

. . . for whatsoever a man soweth, that shall he also reap.

Galations 6:7

What goes around, comes around.

Almost everybody

There it is. That's the Law. The Law of Reciprocity. The Law that says you get back exactly what you give. You might have thought I was going to write about the importance of following the laws of the city, the county, the state or even the federal government. Those laws are indeed important and should be followed. You might have also thought I was going to get preachy and talk to you about following God's law. Those laws are certainly important and should be followed. However, these laws are all a part of the Law of Reciprocity, the Universal Law of Mankind, the Law of Laws.

You may not have heard it referred to as the Law of Reciprocity before, but I'll bet you've heard of the law. It usually gets stated in one of the quotes that I began the chapter with. All of these quotes are saying the very same thing: life is an echo. Whatever you shout out at it, it will be right there to shout back at you. Oh, the grief I could have saved myself if I had only learned and accepted this law earlier in my life. I unconsciously considered myself and my actions an exception to this law. I somehow thought that what I got was independent of what I did. Looking back, I know that I could have been much farther along in all areas of my life if I had only known the power of this law.

Following this law will impact your success more than any other single action you will ever take. Follow this law with your spouse and your marriage will be wonderful. Live this law with your children and the rewards will have untold impact. Heed the law of reciprocity in your business relationships and your customers will love doing business with you. Use the law in all of your relationships with others and the happiness and harmony you experience will amaze you.

The Law of Reciprocity really **is** a law. It is as real and unbending as the Law of Gravity. Go against the Law of Gravity by jumping off a tall building and you'll go splat on the pavement below. Go against the Law of Reciprocity and the consequences are just as devastating.

Teach this law to your children and look for ways to follow it in your own life. Don't bother looking for exceptions or offering yourself excuses. Accept the law for what it is: **THE LAW!** Then **celebrate** the fact that you have the key. You know the answer. Rejoice in the knowing that your rewards are in direct proportion to your service. You never have to wonder again why things are the way they are for you. They are the way they are because of The Law.

Write down your reflections of The Law of Reciprocity and how it has worked in your life:

Chapter Thirty-one

Have Balance

For what shall it profit a man, if he shall gain the whole world, and lose his own soul?

St. Mark 8:36

The most important word in the English language is ***balance.***

Tom Hopkins

Would you be a success if you made a million dollars this year, but lost your health along the way? Would you be a success if you shot par golf, went fishing every weekend, but lost your family? Of course not! Life has to have balance in order to be successful.

I pointed out earlier that your life has several areas:

Career - Business

Social - Civic

Financial

Family

Physical - Health

Mental - Continuing Education

Spiritual

These areas must all have your attention. Just let one get too much attention and you fall out of balance. Therefore, you must have goals in all areas and constantly monitor your life to make sure each area gets its share.

How much is the proper share for each area? **Your best.** Only your best is good enough for any area of your life. Never give yourself or anyone else less than your best. Look again at my definition of success:

> "Success is being all you can be in each area of your life without sacrificing your ability to be all you can be in each and every other area of your life."

Give everything you have to everything you do. And do something in every area of your life each day. Strive for balance while being your best.

Balance is not mediocrity. Mediocrity is having the ability to be a ten, and settling for a five. Some rationalize this as acceptable because it allows them to be a five in other areas. Fives are never acceptable.

This is where the issue of balance becomes confusing. You might say, "I could shoot par golf if I practiced just three hours every week day and all day on Saturday and Sunday. Since I have that ability, doing anything less than that would be mediocrity." That's true if your life was single-faceted; but it's not. Your life has many facets and to spend that much time in one area would sacrifice the others. Since you have chosen to be successful in all areas, you have determined that balance is success. For you, being in balance is being a ten. Your shooting the best golf you can in the time you have alloted , is your **chosen** level of best. That means you are a ten because you achieved your best by choice without sacrificing balance.

Balance is not moderation. I agree with Robert Heinlein's character, Lazurus Long, who said: "Everything in excess, nothing in moderation, moderation is for monks." Long understands my definition of success. Everything gets your best! Each area of your life is lived in excess. When each and every area gets excess, you've got balance!

I love my profession. Nothing feels quite the same as an audience responding to my words. I love my family. There is no pleasure like spending time with my wife and my boys. I love time by myself to read and listen to tapes. I love lots of different things. But none of these things can get ALL of my attention. If it did, then the others would suffer. I don't want any area of my life to suffer, so I give each area my best and make sure that I'm giving my best **in** each area. Balance is my number one priority. Balance with best.

When you have successfully learned to balance all the areas of your life and given each area your best, then you have experienced success!

List the amount of time you spend daily in each of these areas and check for balance. Give yourself credit for quality time as well as quantity.

Career/Business

Social/Civic

Financial

Family

Physical/Health

Mental/Continuing Education

Spiritual

Now answer these questions:

How am I doing?

Do I have balance?

Does each area get my best?

Which areas need work?

What will I do to achieve balance?

How can I give my best?

THIRTY-TWO

Be Thankful

In everything give thanks . . .

I Thessalonians 5:18

The more you are thankful for what you have, the more you will have to be thankful for.

Zig Ziglar

You have to be thankful for what you have while you are on your way to having more. You need to be thankful for who you are while you are on your way to becoming more.

The problem most people seem to have with being thankful is that they don't think they have much to be thankful for. They say, "But look at all of my problems!" We have already discussed the fact that you are always going to have problems. Remember that success is a journey, not a destination. All journeys have problems. But with the journey also comes the satisfaction and the success. So be thankful for the journey; be thankful for not only the four lane highways, but also for the bumps and detours.

So you might say, "Does this mean I have to be thankful **for** the problem?" **NO.** Notice the verse from Thessalonians quoted above. It says, **in** everything give thanks, notice that it doesn't say **for** everything give thanks. That would be unreasonable. There are some proponents of positive thinking who say to go ahead and be thankful for your problems. If you can do that, I am happy for you. I personally have not always been able to be thankful for the problem. What I have been able to do is to be thankful in the situation. There is a difference.

One of the things you can always be thankful for is that the problem isn't any worse than it is. Now you may have said to yourself before, "Things couldn't possibly be worse!" This is a mistake. **Things can always get worse!** Don't make the mistake of issuing a challenge to the world. Because the world just might decide to prove to you that things can get worse. So be thankful that your problem is only as small as it is.

You also need to be thankful for your options. And you always have options. There is never just one right answer. Be thankful for your ability to recognize and explore all of the answers.

Be thankful for our system. The free enterprise system always allows you to have more. That's something we need to be thankful for. Remember that you **always** have the ability to have more because you always have the ability to do and be more.

Let me suggest an exercise that will help you reach a better state of thankfulness and will help you keep a proper perspective on life.

Every day write down at least five things you are thankful for. I write my list in my daily planner. This helps me look at my activities, goals and appointments and at the same time review my "thankful for" list.

When you are doing this, be sure to include the things that are the most important to you and also some of the things you might have been taking for granted. List things like your abilities, your talent, your family, your convictions, your morals, your house, your car, your clothes, and so on.

Don't miss a day to work on your "thankful for" list. If you have to miss something, miss a meal. We can always do with one less meal. We can never do without being thankful!

Start right now by making a list of the things you are most thankful for in your life.

My "thankful for" list:

CHAPTER THIRTY-THREE

What Does It All Mean?

Life is either a daring adventure or it is nothing at all.

Helen Keller

Happiness is getting what you want. Success is wanting what you get.

Unknown

There are two things to aim at in life; First, to get what you want; and after that, to enjoy it. Only the wisest of mankind achieve the second.

Logan Pearsall Smith

You've read the principles - all of my "Simple Ways To Success." So now it is time to ask the question, "What does it all mean?"

It means that none of this is going to work for you. That's right. These principles won't work. In fact, as Charles "Tremendous" Jones says, "Nothing works!"

If you knew of something that worked, then you would just stay home and watch "it" work. But you don't have anything that works. Only you can work. Only you will work. So right now repeat to yourself the following line:

> **!** The greatest plan in the world won't work if you won't.

I stated at the beginning there was nothing magic in the words of this book. I want to repeat that. The magic is not in the words. The magic is in you.

These principles are sound, moral, ethical, smart, solid principles for you to follow and learn from. But don't expect too much from them. The winning difference will not come from this book or any other book. The winning difference is in you. And the good news is that it has always been there. So shake it and wake it and put it to work!

It also means there is risk in putting it all to work. Yes, there is great risk. Not the risk of failing, but the risk of not winning. The risk of not winning is a much greater risk. It means that you have wasted your abilities. You have wasted the talents that are in you. You have **chosen** to be less than you have the potential for being.

It means that you are **obligated** to do and be your best. Anything less than your best means that you've cheated yourself. Not only have you cheated yourself but you've cheated the rest of us. We deserve your best. You deserve your best. Give your best.

I call these principles, "The Simple Way To Success." I often get the question, "Does this really mean that I **have** to do them?" Of course you don't. You don't have to do these things. You can choose to be less than you have the potential for being. You can choose mediocrity. I don't know of anyone, though, who consciously chooses mediocrity. Mediocrity just happens. Don't let it happen to you. Take control of your life **today.** Choose excellence. **Choose success!**

So what does it all mean? If I had to sum it all up in one sentence, it would be:

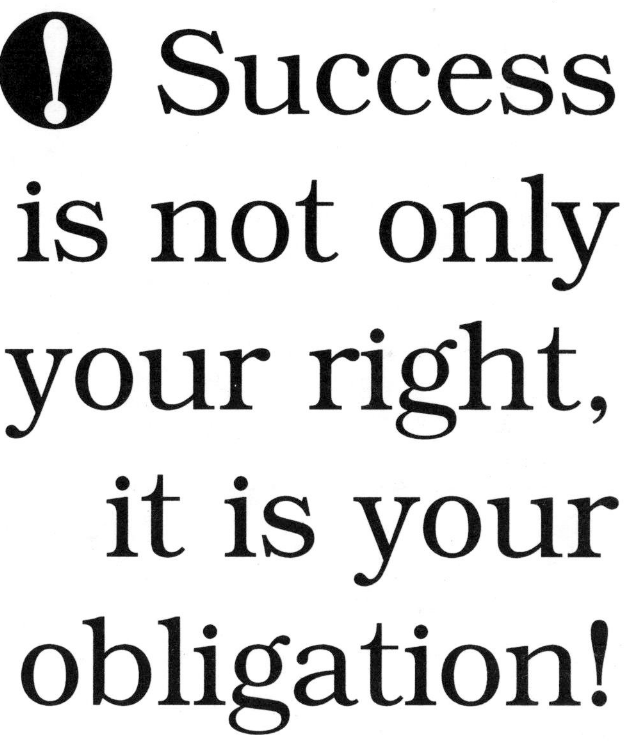

Suggested Reading List

The Bible

Alexander, Scott. **Rhinoceros Success.** Laguna Hills, California: Rhino's Press, 1980.

Anthony, Robert. **Dr. Robert Anthony's Advanced Formula For Total Success.** New York, New York: Berkley Publishing Group, 1988.

Allen, Charles. **God's Psychiatry.** Old Tappan, New Jersey: Fleming H. Revell Company, 1953.

Bettger, Frank. **How I Raised Myself From Failure To Success In Selling.** New York: Prentice Hall Press, 1986.

Brown, W. Steven. **13 Fatal Errors Managers Make And How To Avoid Them.** Old Tappan, New Jersey: Fleming H. Revell Company, 1985.

Clason, George S. **The Richest Man In Babylon.** New York: Hawthorn Books, 1955.

Coffee, Gerald. **Beyond Survival.** New York, New York: G. P. Putnam's Sons, 1990.

DePree, Max. **Leadership Is An Art.** New York, New York: Doubleday, 1989.

Dyer, Wayne. **Real Magic.** New York, New York: HarperCollins Publishers, Inc. 1992

Dyer, Wayne. **You'll See It When You Believe It.** New York, New York: Avon Books, 1989.

Fisher, Mark. **The Instant Millionaire.** San Rafael, California: New World Library, 1990.

Frank, Milo. **How To Get Your Point Across In 30 Seconds Or Less.** New York, N.Y.: Simon & Schuster, Inc., 1986.

Hansen, Mark Victor. **How To Achieve Total Prosperity.** Newport Beach, California: Mark Victor Hansen and Associates, 1981.

Hernacki, Mike. **The Ultimate Secret To Getting Absolutely Everything You Want.** New York, New York: Berkley Publishing Company, 1982.

Hill, Napoleon. **Think And Grow Rich.** North Hollywood, California: Wilshire Book Company, 1966.

Holmes, Ernest. **The Science Of Mind.** New York, New York: G. P. Putnam's Sons, 1938.

Hopkins, Tom. **The Official Guide To Success.** Scottsdale, Arizona: Tom Hopkins International, 1982.

John-Roger and Peter McWilliams. **Wealth 101.** Los Angeles, California: Prelude Press, 1992.

Jones, Charles "Tremendous." **Life Is Tremendous!** Harrisburg, Pennsylvania: Executive Books, 1968

LeBoeuf, Michael. **The Greatest Management Principle In The World.** New York, N.Y.: G. P. Putnam's Sons, 1985.

Mandino, Og. **A Better Way To Live.** New York, New York: Bantam Books, 1990.

Mandino, Og. **The Greatest Salesman In The World.** Hollywood, Florida: Frederick Fell Publishers, Inc., 1968.

Mandino, Og. **Og Mandino's University Of Success.** New York, New York: Bantam Books, 1982.

McGinnis, Alan Loy. **Bringing Out The Best In People.** Minneapolis, Minnesota: Augsburg Publishing House, 1985.

McGinnis, Alan Loy. **The Friendship Factor.** Minneapolis, Minnesota: Augsburg Publishing House, 1979.

Nightingale, Earl. **Earl Nightingale's Greatest Discovery.** New York, New York: Dodd, Mead & Company, Inc., 1987.

Patent, Arnold M. **You Can Have It All.** Sylvia, North Carolina: Celebration Publishing, 1991.

Peale, Norman Vincent. **Positive Imaging.** Old Tappan, New Jersey: Fleming H. Revell Company, 1982.

Peale, Norman Vincent. **Treasury Of Joy And Enthusiasm.** Old Tappan, New Jersey: Fleming H. Revell Co., 1981.

Proctor, Bob. **You Were Born Rich.** Willowdale, Ontario: McCrary Publishing Inc.

Rodgers, Buck. **The IBM Way.** New York, New York: Harper & Row, 1986.

Rodgers, Buck. **Getting The Best Out Of Yourself And Others.** New York, New York: Harper & Row, 1987.

Rohn, Jim. **Seven Strategies For Wealth And Happiness.** Rocklin, California: Prima Publishing & Communications, 1986.

Schuller, Robert H. **Tough Times Don't Last But Tough People Do.** Nashville, Tennessee: Thomas Nelson Publishing, 1983

Schuller, Robert H. **You Can Become The Person You Want To Be.** New York, New York: Elsevier-Dutton, 1973.

Schwartz, David. **The Magic Of Thinking Big.** North Hollywood, California: Wilshire Book Company, 1959.

Waitley, Denis. **Being The Best.** Nashville, Tennessee: Oliver-Nelson Books, 1987.

Waitley, Denis. **Seeds Of Greatness.** Old Tappan, New Jersey: Fleming H.Revell Company, 1983.

Williamson, Marianne. **A Return To Love.** New York, New York: Harper Collins, Inc. 1992.

Ziglar, Zig. **See You At The Top.** Gretna, Louisiana.: Pelican Publishing Company, 1977.

Ziglar, Zig. **Top Performance.** Old Tappan, New Jersey: Fleming H Revell Company, 1986.

This is by no means a complete list and I do not mean to slight any authors or books that are not on the list. This is simply a place to start. If you begin with these books you will find many others along the way that will enrich your life.

"Those are my principles, and if you don't like'em I have more."

Groucho Marx

Larry Winget, CSP

Larry Winget is a philosopher of success who just happens to be hilarious. He teaches universal principles that will work for anyone, in any business, at any time, and does it by telling funny stories. He believes that most of us have complicated life and business way too much, take it way too seriously and that we need to lighten up, take responsibility, be more flexible, stay positive and keep it in perspective. He believes that success and prosperity come from serving others. He teaches that business improves when the people in the business improve; that everything in life gets better when we get better and nothing gets better until we get better.

To have Larry speak to your organization or to order any of his other personal and professional development products contact:

Win Seminars! Inc.
P. O. Box 700485
Tulsa, Oklahoma 74170
918.745.6606
800.749.4597
Fax: 918.747.3185

or use the Internet:
www.larrywinget.com